Simple, Elegant
Pasta Dinners

Simple, Elegant
Pasta Dinners

75 Dishes with *Inspired* Sauces

Nikki Marie

Creator of
Chasing the Seasons

PAGE STREET
PUBLISHING CO.

PAGE STREET
PUBLISHING CO.

For my children,

Giada and Anthony

Table of Contents

SPRING . . . 101

SUMMER . . . 141

"Life is a combination of magic and pasta."

—Federico Fellini

INTRODUCTION

Click, click, vwoom . . . At the sound of gas burners igniting, the kitchen symphony begins. Knives sharpen. Garlic smashes. A hushed stir. The *tap, tap* of a wooden spoon against a skillet. Water runs. Onions sizzle in olive oil, like a round of applause. Dishes clatter. Silverware rustles. Wine breathes. Home cooking is so much more than what we plate and serve—it brings us together, it comforts our soul, it is the music of our roots. Whether it was mom, dad or grandma, it is likely someone in your life played this score for you.

For me, my grandmother was the maestro. Everything I love and learned about cooking happened early on in her tiny kitchen minutes outside of New York City. By way of example, I was introduced the rural-Italian ideology to eat what is locally sourced and to allow the seasons to direct the meal—this became the base of my relationship with food. When I got married in Tuscany and spent some time living and cooking among the locals there, that lifestyle was only reinforced.

Italians cook by way of the ingredients from their own gardens first and then from their local outdoor markets where neighbors sell their proud harvest. They are connoisseurs of fine dining, as they know where the best meals are made—at home. For every family recipe you speak of, they will be certain to counter it with their family's own version.

I came to know a similar lifestyle at 30, when I left the rush of urban life in northern New Jersey, to settle in farther west among the panoramic hills and sweeping fields of Warren County. Just a few minutes in any direction leads to a hard-working family farm with its quaint market and harvest proudly on display. Living here makes it easy to appreciate local agriculture and to savor the fleeting gifts of each season.

While the music of the kitchen and the emerging foods of the seasons have always been part of my fabric, there is a constant ingredient threaded through my life that is still very prominent on my family table.

PASTA.

It is one of the most cost-effective, easy-to-make and versatile ingredients to exist. It plays the part of a main course, a side dish and, yes, even a dessert (take a peek at page 91).

While tried and true pasta recipes, like spaghetti in a long-simmered marinara or traditional lasagna, will always have a permanent place in my recipe repertoire, I wanted to create a cookbook to elevate how we think about and cook with pasta. In this book I offer new possibilities and introduce simple dishes deemed worthy of your best company—all the while remaining as easy as spaghetti and meatballs.

Here's the secret: It is the element of "the unexpected," whether in flavor combinations, ingredients or techniques, that will take a simple and ordinary pasta dish and make it feel like something elegant and special.

If you consider pasta in its most pure state, it is quite plain (in a good way), much like bread. It is precisely this blandness that makes pasta the perfect base for a wide range of unexpectedly delightful flavor combinations. Have you ever roasted summer cherries or autumn grapes and tossed them with pasta? Or grated a heavy and plump tomato for a raw sauce that was so ripe it nearly fell apart in your hands? Oh, and if you've never swapped cooking water for wine, in this book we'll do it twice (page 25 and 64).

Anaïs Nin once said, "We write to taste life twice, in the moment and in retrospection." The same can be said for home cooking, in my opinion. We cook for the moment, of course, but cooking is also a way we recall our past. If you've followed along on my blog, Chasing the Seasons, I have frequently related a memory to a meal or an aroma. These days, cooking is how I reconnect to my grandmother. A simple percolating pot with its rattling lid and tufts of steam will bring me right back to her small kitchen. Suddenly, it's as though I can feel the warmth of her hands, the shape of her petite fingers over mine, as she helps me to carefully stir something on the stove. It's in those moments that our pots are like cauldrons—simmering up nostalgia, invoking the old magic and aching love of days long gone.

So, come with me on a journey where cooking is seasonal and where family, memories and pasta are at the heart.

Writing this cookbook has been an absolute privilege. It sincerely makes me happy and humble to know that the pasta recipes that have storied my life and nourished my family have made their way to your home.

My hope is that you will use this cookbook as a guide, not a rule. Cooking is a personal experience and taste is subjective, so please make these recipes your own. Swap out one ingredient for another or use your favorite type of pasta. Fold down a page corner, ink up the recipes with your own notes and wear out the pages with splats of olive oil and wine. To me, that's a cookbook well loved.

I'll see you in the kitchen.

GETTING STARTED

All Your Pasta Questions Answered
More than just following a recipe, there are a few pasta basics to keep in mind to make a successful dish.

Do Pasta Shapes Matter?
They do. Pasta with texture and shape pairs best with recipes that call for ground meats, vegetables and a thick or saucy essence—it's the texture and shape that will hold to the ingredients, cradling them in their bends and folds. For example, try curly corkscrews, hollow bucatini, pastas with ridges and the scroll-like shape of casarecce and gemelli.

Medium-sized, tubular shapes, like rigatoni and penne, do the same and pair perfectly with thick sauces.

Long, thin pasta like angel hair or linguine work best with lighter oil-based sauces. Thicker strands like fettuccine and pappardelle hold up best when paired with thicker, creamier or meatier sauces. Their broader shapes can withstand the heavier base.

Tiny pastas, like pastina or ditalini, pair best in any spoon-able dish, like brothy soups, or with small chopped ingredients like potatoes with greens or herbs or in a simple butter and oil combination.

How Much Water Does Pasta Need to Boil?
Enough and then some. When making pasta, fresh or dried, you will need a large, deep pot. The idea is to use at least 4 quarts (16 cups [3,785 ml]) of water per 1 pound (454 g) of pasta. This will allow adequate room for the pasta to cook evenly and for adequate stirring to prevent sticking.

When Should You Salt the Water?
When the water boils, and not a moment before. The water in the pot should be at a full, rapid boil when salt is added. Then add the pasta. Adding salt to the water before it comes to a boil will result in some of the salt evaporating while the pot is heating up. Also, forgoing the salt altogether will result in a bland pasta regardless of the salt content in the rest of the recipe. Always add a generous amount: think 1 heaping tablespoon (18 g) of fine kosher salt for 4 quarts (16 cups [3,785 ml]) of water. If using a coarser salt, use 2 tablespoons (35 g) or use 1 tablespoon (18 g) of regular iodized salt.

Should You Add Oil to the Water?
No. While adding oil to the water will prevent the pasta from sticking, it will also leave the pasta slick, and the intended sauce will be less likely to adhere to the pasta.

How Can You Prevent Pasta from Sticking?

In short, with ample water and frequent stirring. It's really that simple. Longer pasta (such as fettuccine, spaghetti, etc.) will need just a few seconds to soften before stirring. Medium and small pasta should be stirred immediately. The initial stir shouldn't be too brief either, as newly submerged pasta will naturally want to adhere. Factor on initially stirring for at least 15 to 20 continuous seconds to ensure that each piece of pasta is thoroughly wet, moving around and beginning to soften. Then, continue to stir often until the pasta is ready.

What is "Al Dente"?

Al dente literally means "to the tooth" in Italian. If using store-bought pasta, use the cooking time on the package as a guide and then taste the pasta—that's really the only way to truly determine if it is ready. It should be tender, yet slightly firm to the bite. Because most pasta dishes will finish cooking in a hot skillet, pasta should be boiled until it is molto al dente, "very much to the tooth"—about 1 to 2 minutes before it is considered perfectly al dente. Why? Because adding perfectly al dente pasta to a hot skillet will cause it to become overcooked as it continues to toss with whatever hot contents await. The same rule applies for pasta that will finish baking in the oven. On the flip side, if you are ready to plate your pasta and the inner core is gritty and white, it's undercooked and needs to be cooked for a little longer.

Should You Rinse Cooked Pasta?

Never, and yes. It depends on how the pasta will be used. In hot pasta dishes, the thin layer of starch on pasta acts like a glue and is necessary to help the sauce stick to the pasta. Rinsing that off would compromise the integrity of the dish—unless of course, you're making a cold pasta dish or a stir-fry. Then rinsing is necessary to eliminate that layer of starch that would otherwise create a gummy and pasty dish. There's a caveat here, though, when it comes to soups. Some creamy soups need the starch and so the pasta cooks in the soup from the very beginning, while other, brothier soups benefit from separately cooked and slightly rinsed pasta before adding.

Do You Really Need to Reserve the Cooked Pasta Water?

Always! It's liquid gold! Pasta water is filled with starch and when it is added to hot oil or butter at the end of cooking, it will emulisfy the sauce. Pasta water is the key to a silky and smooth end result. Even if you think you don't need it, save at least a cup or two (240–480 ml), unless a specific recipe calls for more. To keep it simple, I use a large measuring cup that holds approximately 4–5 cups (960–1,200 ml) and carefully submerge it into the pot of water before draining. I use what is needed to help emulsify the oil or sauce, or loosen the pasta, and discard what I don't need.

Here's a tip: *Keep extra pasta water on the side until the meal has been finished. Having the extra water on hand will help to reconstitute a dish that has sat out a little longer than anticipated, especially when family doesn't all eat at the same time.*

Making Fresh Pasta? There Is a Right Way to Measure Flour

Improperly measured flour will yield a flavorless or ruined recipe. Never scoop flour out of a container or bag. Doing so will pack the flour, adding much more to the recipe than required. Instead, lightly spoon the flour directly into a proper measuring cup. Do not shake or tap the cup, this will also pack the flour. Continue to spoon until the flour mounds above the cup. Then, using the nonserrated side of a kitchen knife, very lightly sweep away the excess flour. Do this until the flour is level, still taking care not to shake or tap the cup. An accurate cup of flour should weigh 125 grams.

How to Store Fresh Pasta

While dried pastas can be stored in the boxes or bags they are purchased in, or inside of an airtight canister, fresh pasta is a little different. Depending on the ingredients used in the pasta, the storing methods will differ. A fresh pasta that consists of only flour and water can be stored at room temperature after it has been thoroughly dried—noting that if any moisture remains, mold will develop—so take care to make certain the pasta has dried before storing.

Any other type of fresh pasta can be cooked right away or left to dry out for a few minutes, dusted with flour to prevent sticking, and then gently folded into nests. Continue to let the nests dry for another 30 minutes; then wrap and refrigerate for 2 days or freeze for up to 2 weeks.

A stuffed pasta, like ravioli, should be partially frozen right on the baking trays they rest on before storing—just pop the tray right into the freezer! Once partially frozen, the ravioli can be transferred into large freezer-safe storage bags. Note that frozen ravioli will take a little longer to cook.

Basic Pasta Dough

To make fresh pasta, you will need flour and water, and in most, but not all cases, eggs. Italian doppio zero "00" flour, found in Italian specialty stores, or in Italy itself, will provide the most refined, silkiest pasta. An all-purpose flour will result in a more full-bodied pasta. Either is perfectly fine. Keep in mind that flour will absorb moisture differently depending on its age and the humidity of the kitchen. Therefore, always keep extra flour and water on hand. If the dough is too sticky, dust with more flour; too dry, add a little more water. Start with the measurements below and then use your judgment. I prefer using the traditional well method as this will ensure the most even mix. To roll and cut the pasta, I use a hand-cranked pasta machine, unless otherwise noted.

Serves 4–6

3½ cups (438 g) "00" flour or all-purpose flour, plus approximately ½ cup (62 g) for kneading

¼ tsp kosher salt

4 eggs

1 tbsp (15 ml) extra-virgin olive oil

Mound the 3½ cups (438 g) of flour in the middle of a flat work surface. Mix the salt into the flour with a fork. Make a hole, or a well, in the center of the flour large enough to accommodate the eggs while keeping the walls of the well thick enough so the eggs will not spill out from beyond the well walls.

Slowly pour the eggs into the well along with the olive oil. If using any special additions like herbs or purees, add them now.

Using a fork, slowly beat the eggs and gradually begin to incorporate more flour from the sides, always starting with the flour that is closest to the egg mixture. Continue to beat, adding even more flour, sometimes using your other hand to help push up and retain the outer wall of flour. Halfway through this process, you will notice the flour and egg mixture turn pasty and the eggs will no longer have a chance to run. At this point you can put the fork aside and use the heels of your hands to form a shaggy mass of dough. Just lightly knead at this point, and if the dough is sticking to your hands, add more flour.

Putting the mound of dough to the side, scrape up and discard any dried bits of flour from your work surface and hands. Wash your hands and dry them well. Lightly flour your work surface again and, relying on Italian chef Marcella Hazan's method here, stick your thumb deep into the mound of dough; if it comes out clean without any sticky remnants, no more flouring is needed. If still too sticky, add more flour.

Continue to knead the dough. Kneading the dough by hand is a key component to homemade pasta. To properly knead, use the heels of your palms. Use your fingertips only to pull the dough toward you, giving it a half turn counterclockwise, and press down hard again with the heels of your palms, pushing your body weight into the dough. Continue this process for about 10 minutes, kneading and turning.

After kneading, the dough should be elastic and smooth. Form the dough into a disc shape, or ball, and wrap it in plastic wrap. Allow the dough to rest for 30 minutes at room temperature, to help the gluten relax, before rolling it out or shaping it as desired.

After 30 minutes, unwrap the dough and knead it a few times to work in any moisture that has formed. The dough should feel smooth and silky.

Using a sharp knife, cut the dough into eight equal pieces. Work with one piece at a time; wrap the rest in plastic wrap until ready.

Flatten the piece of dough in your hand as best as possible, then run it through the rollers of your pasta machine at the widest setting, the lowest number, usually "1." If it is sticky, dust it with more flour.

Fold the rolled piece of dough by bringing the two ends to meet in the center and run it through the rollers again with the folds perpendicular to the rollers. Fold the dough the same way again and run it through the rollers one more time, again dusting with more flour if the dough feels sticky as it thins.

Lightly dust the rolled dough with flour and place it onto a clean, dry sheet or towel. Proceed with the remaining pieces of dough in the exact same way.

After all the pieces have been run through the machine at the widest setting, adjust the rollers one notch, to the next number up, and put each piece of dough through just once—there's no need to fold anymore. Again, dust with flour if needed. Repeat with each piece of dough, going up one notch at time, narrowing the rollers, until you reach the desired setting, usually number "4"—you won't want dough that is too thin as it will need to withstand cooking. Cut the sheets of pasta in half by hand if they get too long.

To use the pasta machine cutter, first cut the pasta sheets by hand into lengths approximately 15 inches (38 cm) long. Always start with the first piece of dough that was rolled out and run it through the desired cutting attachment. The attachment with the larger cutters is for fettuccine and the smaller ones for spaghetti. Gently lay the cut pasta onto clean cotton towels or a sheet and dust lightly again with flour. Proceed with the desired recipe.

Prepare the well.

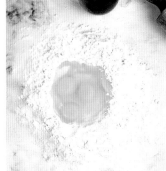
Add the eggs and oil.

Beat the eggs and carefully draw in more flour.

Create a cohesive, shaggy mass of dough.

Knead the dough.

The dough should be silky and smooth before resting.

"Everything you see I owe to spaghetti."
—Sophia Loren

AUTUMN

For me, autumn is official when the orchards are ripe for apple picking, usually right before the changing leaves begin to carpet the ground. I bid farewell to summer's offerings and transition to autumn cooking, leaning first on the sweet apples of the season—they're not just for baking! Slightly cooked apples retain a subtle bite and their succulent sweetness twists and tangles in long tendrils of pasta in a savory dish like Bucatini with Cider, Caramelized Onions and Honeycrisp Apples (page 21).

As the days become crisp and short and the evening wine flows to keep the warmth in our cheeks, my cooking techniques and preferences adjust too. I might even swap my cooking water for wine, steeping par-cooked spaghetti in a hot aromatic pot of my favorite red for a dinner that is simple to prepare yet tastes like a Tuscan memory in my Red Wine Spaghetti with Swiss Chard (page 25).

With mushrooms abounding, we take our baskets in hand and forage the woods. There's something about going deep into the woods that's enchanting. Though we aren't always successful, sometimes it is the magic of the woods that leads us, and we find our wild treasures under crisp fallen leaves. Cooking with mushrooms is bewitching to me, whether I've foraged for them myself or purchased them. I use them in a variety of autumnal dishes like Baked Shells with Fresh Ricotta, Caramelized Onions and Wild Mushrooms (page 34) and Ravioli with Port Wine and Mushroom Sauce (page 22).

The season is abundant with fresh herbs, too. The sage I harvested all summer long is lush and thriving, enticing me with its earthy aroma, and I seek ways to capture its essence as a main ingredient. Have you ever added freshly snipped sage to homemade pasta dough? It's such a simple way to transform traditional dough into a lightly green-speckled and fragrant pasta in Fresh Sage Fettuccine with Brown Butter (page 55).

I'd be remiss though if I didn't include autumn's lesser-thought-of goodies too, like red grapes. When roasted, they caramelize just so, and their sweet nectar deepens and intensifies. I like to add them to dress up a simple casarecce and sausage dish, balancing their bursting sweetness with a creamy bite of Gorgonzola in Pasta with Sausage and Roasted Red Grapes (page 29).

If I had to pick just one dish that offers a little sampling of autumn's finest, I'd choose my Autumn Harvest Lasagna (page 37), layered with butternut squash, local kale and thinly sliced hand-picked apples cloaked in a homemade béchamel sauce.

Autumn is a magical time. Cooking is slower and there's an array of hearty ingredients to choose from—all in the colors of the changing landscape and falling leaves. The pages that follow will give you a glimpse into the plentiful ways to pair these ingredients with pasta.

Bucatini with Cider, Caramelized Onions and Honeycrisp Apples

In the region of Trentino, in Northern Italy, where apple orchards abound, apples have long been enjoyed in savory dishes. I've combined a good heat-tolerant apple, Honeycrisp, with deeply caramelized onions, a splash of dry white wine and cider. I prefer to use a longer, full-bodied pasta like bucatini, capturing a bit of the apples and sweet onions with every twist and twirl of my fork. This is one of my family's favorite autumnal pasta dishes, taking full advantage of apples at their peak, both in harvest and in taste.

Serves 4–6

Kosher salt

1 lb (454 g) bucatini

5 tbsp (60 ml) extra-virgin olive oil, divided, plus more if needed

2 tbsp (30 g) butter

4 oz (112 g) diced pancetta

2 large Vidalia onions, halved and sliced about ¼ inch (6 mm) thick

¼ tsp ground cloves

Freshly ground pepper, to taste

⅔ cup (160 ml) Sauvignon Blanc

½ cup (120 ml) local or quality apple cider

3 medium Honeycrisp apples, peeled, cored and diced

10 sage leaves, to garnish

Grated Parmigiano-Reggiano or local cheese with a hard and sharp profile, to garnish

Bring a large pot of water to a boil. Generously salt the water, then add the pasta. Cook until just shy of al dente, tender yet firm to the bite, according to the package directions. Reserve 1 cup (240 ml) of the pasta water before draining. Drain well.

Meanwhile, in a large 12-inch (30-cm) skillet with deep sides, over low–medium heat, add 4 tablespoons (60 ml) of olive oil and butter. When the oil is hot and the butter is melted, add the pancetta and toss until almost crisp, 5 to 6 minutes. Use a slotted spoon to transfer the pancetta to a separate bowl and set aside.

Add the onions to the skillet, seasoning with the cloves and salt and freshly ground pepper to taste. Stir to combine. Sauté, stirring often, until the onions are tender and deeply caramelized, 25 to 30 minutes, lowering the heat if necessary to prevent the oil from smoking. Use a slotted spoon to remove the onions and transfer them to the same bowl as the pancetta.

Remove the skillet from the heat and add the wine and cider. Return to a high heat and boil. Deglaze the pan by scraping up any flavorful brown bits that may have accumulated. Cook until the wine and cider have reduced just a bit, about 5 minutes.

Add the apples to the skillet. Season with salt and pepper, and stir to combine. Lower the heat and simmer the apples until they are tender but with a slight bite, 5 to 10 minutes. Be careful not to overcook the apples; they should have a subtle, soft bite and not be mushy.

In the meantime, prepare the fried sage leaves. Add 1 tablespoon (15 ml) of olive oil to a small pan and fry the leaves until crisp, 1 to 2 minutes. Transfer to a plate lined with a paper towel to absorb the excess oil. Set aside.

Add the cooked pasta to the skillet along with ¼ cup (60 ml) of the reserved pasta water and toss together to combine, 1 minute. If needed, use more reserved water, a little at a time, to loosen the pasta—the pasta should have movement and not be pasty or sticky. Add the onions and pancetta back to the skillet and toss well to incorporate.

To serve, divide onto individual plates and drizzle lightly with extra-virgin olive oil, fresh pepper, grated cheese and fried sage leaves.

Ravioli with Port Wine and Mushroom Sauce

Autumn calls for deep flavors, textures and aromas that nourish the body and comfort the soul. In this recipe, mushrooms are fragrant with rosemary and the intricate fruit flavors and spices of a fine ruby port, creating the perfect essence for a plate of piping hot ravioli. Be sure to serve with a good crusty bread to mop up the sauce that is left on your plate (that's my favorite part). This sauce alone is worth bookmarking as it doubles as a gorgeous companion to steak or roasted chicken.

Serves 4–6

2 tsp (6 g) cornstarch

1 cup (240 ml) plus 2 tsp (10 ml) vegetable broth, divided

Kosher salt

1 lb 9 oz (708 g) ravioli

½ cup (115 g) butter

1 large shallot, thinly sliced

8 oz (227 g) baby bella mushrooms, ends trimmed and thinly sliced

1 tsp finely chopped rosemary

Freshly ground pepper, to taste

½ cup (120 ml) fine ruby port

Grated Parmigiano–Reggiano or local cheese with a hard and sharp profile, to garnish

In a small bowl, make a slurry with the cornstarch and 2 teaspoons (10 ml) of room temperature or cold broth. Stir well, making a thin, watery paste, and set aside.

Bring a large pot of water to a boil. Generously salt the water and add the ravioli. Cook according to the package directions. Reserve ¼ cup (60 ml) of the pasta water before draining. Drain well.

In the meantime, in a large 12-inch (30-cm) skillet with deep sides over medium heat, melt the butter. Add the shallot, mushrooms and rosemary, and season with salt and a few turns of freshly ground pepper, stirring well to coat the mushrooms. Cook, stirring often, until the shallots soften and the mushrooms are tender, about 10 minutes.

Remove the skillet from the heat to add the port. Scrape the bottom of the pan to deglaze any flavorful brown bits that may have accumulated. Raise the heat to high and bring the wine to a full boil; then allow it to reduce almost completely, stirring occasionally, until it just barely covers the shallots in a little more than a glaze, 5 to 7 minutes. Add 1 cup (240 ml) of the vegetable broth and stir to combine. Bring the broth to a boil, and then reduce the heat to a simmer. Add the slurry and stir continuously to combine.

Continue to cook, raising the heat if necessary, to thicken the sauce just a bit, 1 to 2 minutes. The consistency should be a flavorful essence, not quite as thick as a gravy, though not watery either. If you can run your spoon through the pan and see some separation before the sauce runs back together, it's perfect. Turn off the heat. Taste and adjust the seasonings if necessary.

Add the cooked ravioli to the skillet and gently fold the sauce over the ravioli to combine. Add the reserved pasta water, 1 tablespoon (15 ml) at a time, if you need to thin the sauce a bit further.

Serve hot with freshly grated cheese and a good rustic bread to soak up that flavorful essence.

Red Wine Spaghetti with Swiss Chard

I first encountered spaghetti cooked in red wine while escaping the rain in Tuscany. It was the most luxurious pasta I had ever had. I thought for sure that I must have died and heaven was an osteria, where Jesus turned pasta water into wine, and my angel was an Italian nonna. I thought about it often but never came across a recipe for it until a few years ago in the New York Times. *This is my version inspired by Alessandro Giuntoli's recipe. The wine imparts a deep burgundy hue to the pasta and the flavors of the wine are absorbed. While you won't need to splurge on an expensive bottle of wine, it should be a wine that you like as the flavors of the wine are key.*

Serves 4–6

½ cup (120 ml) extra-virgin olive oil, plus more for drizzling

2 cloves garlic, smashed and cut in half (leaving the pieces large enough to remove later)

1 bunch Swiss chard, washed, center stems discarded, leaves chopped into bite-sized pieces

1 small onion, thinly sliced

Kosher salt

2 tbsp (30 g) tomato paste

1 (25-oz [740-ml]) bottle of Italian red wine (like Toscana or Chianti), divided

1 lb (454 g) spaghetti

½ cup (120 ml) chicken broth

Freshly ground pepper, to taste

1 tbsp (15 g) butter

Freshly grated pecorino cheese, to garnish

Bring a large pot of water to a boil. (Note that you'll be working with the pot of boiling water and a large 13- to 15-inch (33- to 38-cm) skillet with deep sides on the stove at the same time.)

Add the olive oil to the skillet over medium heat. When the oil is hot and shimmery, add the garlic. Stir until fragrant, 30 seconds. Add the Swiss chard and sauté until tender and bright green, 1 to 2 minutes. Remove the chard from the skillet using a slotted spoon and set aside, reserving the olive oil and garlic in the skillet.

Add the sliced onion to the skillet and lightly sprinkle with salt. Sauté, stirring often, until the onions are tender and beginning to caramelize, 10 minutes. When the garlic has lightly browned, remove it with a slotted spoon and discard.

Add the tomato paste to the onions and allow the paste to sit in the center of the skillet, the hottest part, and caramelize, about 3 minutes. Then stir to incorporate with the onions.

When the water is boiling, generously salt, then add ¼ cup (60 ml) of red wine and the spaghetti. Stir frequently to prevent sticking and until some of the starch has cooked out from the pasta, 5 to 6 minutes. At this point the pasta should be very bendable, though still undercooked. Reserve 1 cup (240 ml) of the pasta water before draining. Drain well.

In the meantime, remove the skillet from the heat and add the remainder of the bottle of red wine, scraping the bottom of the skillet to deglaze any flavorful brown bits that may have accumulated. Return to a high heat and add the broth, ¼ cup (60 ml) of the reserved pasta water and the par-cooked spaghetti. Season with salt and pepper. Let the mixture come to a low boil, stirring frequently to prevent sticking, about 6 minutes. Taste. Spaghetti should be al dente: tender yet firm to the bite. If not, continue to boil for another minute and taste again. Use the remaining pasta water only if needed to help loosen the pasta. The pasta should be silky, not sticky. Turn off the heat and add the butter, then toss gently.

Add the Swiss chard to the skillet and toss to combine. Drizzle each serving with extra-virgin olive oil and ribbons of pecorino cheese. Serve immediately.

Caramelized Purple Cabbage with Egg Noodles

While this recipe leans mostly toward being a side dish, it can also be a satisfying light lunch or dinner, especially when paired with pork, some greens and a good crusty bread. Using the purple cabbage of autumn is aesthetically pleasing and makes for a beautiful table presentation.

Serves 4–6

Kosher salt

1 lb (454 g) egg noodles

½ cup (115 g) butter

1 medium onion, thinly sliced

1 small head cabbage (about 11 oz [312 g]), cored, and cut into 1-inch (2.5-cm) pieces

Freshly ground pepper, to taste

2 cloves garlic, finely grated

½ cup (120 ml) vegetable broth

Bring a large pot of water to a boil. Generously salt and then add the pasta. Cook until just shy of al dente, tender yet firm to the bite, according to the package directions. Reserve ½ cup (120 ml) of the pasta water before draining. Drain well.

In the meantime, add the butter to a large 12-inch (30-cm) skillet with deep sides over low–medium heat. When the butter is melted, add the onion and cabbage and lightly sprinkle with salt and a few turns of freshly ground pepper. Cook, stirring often, until the onion and cabbage become tender and lightly caramelized, 15 to 20 minutes. Add the garlic, stirring until fragrant, 30 seconds.

Add the vegetable broth to the skillet and stir well to combine, scraping the bottom of the skillet to deglaze any flavorful brown bits that may have accumulated. Continue to stir until heated through, 2 minutes.

Add the pasta and ¼ cup (60 ml) of the reserved pasta water. Lower to a simmer for another minute, until the liquids have slightly reduced. Taste and adjust the seasonings, if necessary. Only use the remaining reserved pasta water to help loosen the pasta if needed.

To serve, divide into individual bowls, garnish with pepper and serve hot or at room temperature.

Pasta with Sausage and Roasted Red Grapes

This simple dish is an early autumn favorite when I want to add interest to an otherwise easy weeknight dinner. September and October marks the start of the grape harvest. While most of New Jersey's grapes are harvested for wine, varieties of fresh grapes begin to fill the farm markets, and I have a penchant for roasting them. Roasting deepens their flavor and adds a burst of warm sweetness that complements ground sausage beautifully. The perfect scrolled shape of the casarecce cradles the flavors, and the sweet and savory elements are perfectly balanced by the salty bite of Gorgonzola.

Serves 4—6

⅓–½ lb (151–225 g) red grapes, stems discarded

¼ cup (60 ml) plus 1 tbsp (15 ml) extra-virgin olive oil, divided

Kosher salt and freshly ground pepper, to taste

1 lb (454 g) casarecce (or any other medium-cut pasta, like gemelli)

1 medium onion, diced

10 fresh sage leaves, to garnish

1 lb (454 g) sweet Italian sausage, preground or whole with casings removed

1 large clove garlic, finely grated

1 cup (240 ml) vegetable broth

Gorgonzola cheese, crumbled, to garnish

Preheat the oven to 375°F (190°C).

Line a baking sheet with parchment paper or a silicone mat and spread the grapes out on the sheet. Drizzle with 1 tablespoon (15 ml) of olive oil, season with salt and pepper and evenly massage over and around the grapes. Roast the grapes for 15 to 20 minutes or until they begin to split and burst. Set aside to cool.

Bring a large pot of water to a boil. Generously salt the water, then add the pasta. Cook until the pasta is just shy of al dente: tender yet firm to the bite, according to the package directions. Reserve ½ cup (120 ml) of the pasta water before draining. Drain well.

In the meantime, in a large 12-inch (30-cm) skillet with deep sides over medium heat, add ¼ cup (60 ml) of olive oil. When the oil is hot and shimmery, add the onion, lightly sprinkle with salt (noting that the sausage will add a measure of saltiness) and sauté, stirring often, until almost tender, 5 minutes.

Slide the onion to the sides of the pan and carefully add the sage leaves to the center of the skillet. Be careful when adding them, as they tend to pop and splatter when fried. Cook the sage leaves for about 1 minute or until they begin to crisp (they'll continue to crisp as they cool). Use tongs or a slotted spoon to transfer the sage to a paper towel–lined plate and set aside.

Add the sausage and garlic to the onions. If removing the casings from the whole sausage, break it up into ground/bite-sized pieces with your cooking spoon or a fork. Continue to cook, stirring frequently, until all the sausage is lightly browned and no longer pink inside and the onions are tender and carmelized, about 10 minutes. Add the vegetable broth and bring to a boil, then reduce to a simmer, deglazing the pan by scraping up any brown bits that have accumulated.

Add the pasta and ¼ cup (60 ml) of the reserved pasta water to the skillet. Toss well to combine and to allow the pasta to absorb most, but not all, of the liquid, 1 minute. If needed, add the rest of the pasta water and a drizzle of olive oil to help loosen the pasta.

To serve, divide into individual bowls and top each serving with the desired amount of Gorgonzola, crispy sage leaves (whole or broken) and a sprinkle of roasted grapes.

French Onion Penne

To highlight the onion harvest, I'm giving onions the leading role in this comforting autumn dish, a quick and easy pasta version of French onion soup, complete with the familiar flavor of onions sweetened in red wine and broth. Snips of fresh rosemary enhance the layers of melted Gruyere and mozzarella cheese. I chose penne as it is one of my favorite pastas to use in a baked dish, with its hollowed core acting like a vessel, capturing all that ooey-gooey goodness that completes a chilly autumn evening.

Serves 4–6

Kosher salt

1 lb (454 g) penne (ziti would work well too)

2 tbsp (30 ml) extra-virgin olive oil

4 tbsp (60 g) butter

3 medium yellow onions, halved then sliced about ¼ inch (6 mm) thick

Freshly ground pepper, to taste

1 large clove garlic, finely grated

1 cup (240 ml) dry red wine

1½ tsp (3 g) finely chopped fresh rosemary leaves, center stem discarded

2 tbsp (16 g) all-purpose, unbleached flour

2½ cups (600 ml) beef stock

½ cup (120 ml) whole milk

6½ oz (190 g) shredded Gruyere cheese

1–1½ cups (112–168 g) shredded mozzarella

Bring a large pot of water to a boil. Generously salt the water and add the pasta. Cook the pasta until it is 2 to 3 minutes shy of al dente, tender yet firm to the bite, according to the package directions.

In the meantime, in a large (roughly 5-quart [4.7-L]) enameled cast-iron pot over medium–high heat, warm the olive oil and butter. When the oil is hot and shimmery, and the butter is beginning to foam, add the onions and season lightly with salt and pepper. Sauté, stirring often, until tender and beginning to caramelize, 10 to 15 minutes. Add the garlic, cooking and stirring until fragrant, 30 seconds.

Remove the pot from the heat, then add the wine and rosemary. Return the pot to moderate heat and let the wine cook until it has reduced almost completely, leaving behind a silky essence to coat the onions, about 10 minutes. If the pasta is not done yet, it's fine to turn off the heat under the onions. When the pasta is ready, be sure to bring the onions back to a full simmer before proceeding; the pot will need to be hot to continue.

Sprinkle the flour over the onions and stir well to incorporate. Gradually whisk in the beef stock and bring to a boil. Cook for 1 minute more. Season to taste with salt and pepper. Lower the heat to a simmer, then add the pasta and stir to mix well.

Stir in the milk and Gruyere cheese. Continue stirring to mix well and to thoroughly melt the cheese. Remove from the heat and sprinkle the top evenly with mozzarella. Set the broiler to high and place the pot under the broiler until the mozzarella is melted, 3 to 5 minutes—keeping a watchful eye as broiler temperatures vary.

Allow the pot to sit for 5 to 10 minutes before serving, to allow the mixture to thicken a bit.

Cook's Notes: *If the mozzarella is too soft to shred, pop it in the freezer for a few minutes.*

Spaghetti with Parmigiano-Roasted Cauliflower

Our local farmers, the Donaldson family, grow the most beautiful jewel-toned cauliflower in shades of deep amethyst, yellow and creamy white. I always grab a few, even if I already have some at home. In this recipe, the florets are roasted, seasoned with toasted Parmigiano and tossed with hot tendrils of spaghetti.

Serves 4–6

2 medium heads of cauliflower, outer leaves discarded, stems trimmed, divided into florets

¼ cup (60 ml) plus 2 tbsp (30 ml) extra-virgin olive oil, divided, plus more as needed

Kosher salt and freshly ground pepper, to taste

¼ tsp red pepper flakes, plus more for optional garnish

¼ cup (25 g) finely grated Parmigiano-Reggiano, plus more to garnish

1 lb (454 g) spaghetti

1 medium onion, thinly sliced

1 cup (240 ml) vegetable broth

Preheat the oven to 450°F (230°C).

Line a large baking sheet with parchment paper. Spread the cauliflower florets on the sheet and drizzle with 2 tablespoons (30 ml) of olive oil. Massage the oil over and around the florets, adding more oil if needed, to evenly coat. Season well with salt, pepper and red pepper flakes.

Roast, tossing once halfway through, until the stems can be easily pierced with a fork, about 20 minutes. At the halfway mark, sprinkle the florets evenly with Parmigiano-Reggiano. When finished cooking, remove from the oven and set aside.

Bring a large pot of water to a boil. Generously salt the water, then add the pasta. Cook until just shy of al dente, tender yet firm to the bite, according to the package directions. Reserve 1 cup (240 ml) of the pasta water before draining. Drain well.

Meanwhile, in a large 12-inch (30-cm) skillet with deep sides, heat ¼ cup (60 ml) of olive oil over low–medium heat. When the oil is hot and shimmery, add the onion and lightly season with salt. Sauté, stirring often, until the onions are tender and beginning to caramelize, about 10 minutes.

Add the vegetable broth to the onions and cook, deglazing the pan by scraping up any flavorful browned bits that may have accumulated. Continue to cook, 2 minutes. Turn off the heat.

Add the pasta to the skillet with the onions and broth and toss together until most, though not all, of the liquid has been absorbed, 1 to 2 minutes. Add ¼ cup (60 ml) of the reserved pasta water along with the roasted cauliflower, and any pieces of toasted Parmigiano that may have stuck to the parchment paper, and toss again.

Add more of the reserved pasta water if the pasta needs to be loosened, ¼ cup (60 ml) at a time, tossing until the desired consistency is reached. Pasta should be silky, have movement and not be sticky. Taste and adjust the seasonings if necessary.

To serve, divide among individual bowls, garnish with freshly ground pepper or more red pepper flakes (or both!) and grated cheese.

Baked Shells with Fresh Ricotta, Caramelized Onions and Wild Mushrooms

Jumbo pasta shells are lightly stuffed with fresh ricotta that has been slightly perfumed with nutmeg. A mixture of caramelized onions, seasonal mushrooms, Swiss chard and fontina are layered on top for an earthy, woodsy take on a classic. If you've never made fresh ricotta before, give it a try! It's easier than you think; it requires only a few kitchen staples and takes about 30 minutes from start to finish. Fresh ricotta is far superior to any store-bought brand and can even be made a few days in advance. However, if you're in a hurry, quality store-bought ricotta will certainly do.

Serves 4

Fresh Ricotta
4 cups (1 L) whole milk
2 cups (480 ml) heavy cream
1 tsp kosher salt
3 tbsp (45 ml) white wine vinegar

To make the homemade ricotta cheese, set a large colander or sieve over a slightly smaller, deep bowl. Set aside.

Dampen two layers of cheesecloth with water and line the colander. Set aside.

Add the milk, heavy cream and salt to a heavy-bottomed saucepan. Cook over moderate heat, stirring occasionally, until the contents come to a full, rapid boil. Turn off the heat and remove the saucepan from it. Stirring gently, add the vinegar, then set aside for 1 to 2 minutes to allow the curds to form—you'll know when they've formed when solids appear in the pot. The curds should be thick enough to not drain through the cheesecloth.

Ladle the hot mixture into the cheesecloth-lined colander and let it stand for 20 to 25 minutes so the whey (the milky water) can drain into the bowl below the colander. Check the bowl periodically; if it is filling up too much, simply gather the cheesecloth in a bundle and pour off the contents of the bowl underneath. Put the colander back over the bowl and continue to drain the cheese. The longer the mixture sits, the thicker the ricotta cheese. If the cheese is thicker than you'd like it to be, add a little bit of milk and stir to mix well.

Reserve 1½ cups (370 g) of the ricotta cheese for this recipe. Spoon the rest into a large jar or container. Discard the cheesecloth and whey. Fresh ricotta cheese can be refrigerated for up to 5 days.

(continued)

Baked Shells with Fresh Ricotta, Caramelized Onions and Wild Mushrooms (Continued)

Baked Shells

4 tbsp (60 g) butter, divided

1½ cups (370 g) fresh ricotta cheese (or substitute with good-quality store-bought)

1 large egg, beaten

¼ cup (60 ml) light cream

½ cup (50 g) grated Parmigiano-Reggiano

¼ tsp ground nutmeg

Kosher salt and freshly ground pepper, to taste

8 oz (227 g) mushrooms, any meaty type, wild or cultivated, cleaned and sliced ¼ inch (6 mm) thick

4 sprigs fresh rosemary

4 tbsp (60 ml) extra-virgin olive oil, divided

12 oz (340 g) jumbo pasta shells

1 large onion, sliced about ¼ inch (6 mm) thick

1 bunch Swiss chard (4–5 stalks), center stems discarded, leaves chopped into bite-sized pieces

1 clove garlic, finely grated

8 oz (227 g) fontina cheese, grated

Preheat the oven to 425°F (220°C) and grease a 9 x 13-inch (23 x 33-cm) baking dish with about 2 tablespoons (30 g) of butter and set aside.

To make the shells, add the ricotta, egg, light cream, grated cheese and nutmeg to a large bowl. Season well with salt and pepper. Mix and set aside.

Line a large baking sheet with parchment paper. Spread the mushrooms on the baking sheet. Add the rosemary sprigs. Drizzle with 2 tablespoons (30 ml) of olive oil, season to taste with salt and pepper and gently massage onto the mushrooms and rosemary. Roast, tossing once, until golden and tender, 10 to 15 minutes. Remove the crispy rosemary leaves from their branches and mix them with the mushrooms, then discard the branches. Set the mixture aside. Raise the oven temperature to 450°F (230°C).

Bring a large pot of water to a boil. Generously salt and then add the pasta. Cook 2 to 3 minutes shy of al dente, tender yet firm to the bite, according to the package directions. Drain well.

In the meantime, in a 12-inch (30-cm) skillet over low–medium heat, add 2 tablespoons (30 ml) of olive oil and the remaining 2 tablespoons (30 g) of butter. When the oil is hot and the butter is melted, add the onion. Lightly sprinkle with salt and sauté, stirring often, until tender and caramelized, 10 minutes. Add the Swiss chard and sauté until wilted, 2 to 3 minutes. Add the garlic and sauté until fragrant, 30 seconds. Remove the skillet from the heat and set aside.

Arrange the shells in the buttered baking dish. Working with one shell at a time, fill the shells a little more than halfway with the ricotta mixture—spillovers are welcomed and overlapping the shells is fine. Any leftover mixture should be spooned into the baking dish around the shells. Dollop the top of the shells with the onion and chard mixture, roughly spreading it out, and drizzle with any residual oil and butter from the skillet.

Top with the mushroom mixture and fontina, spreading the cheese out evenly over the mushrooms and pasta. Bake until the cheese is melted and bubbly, 10 to 15 minutes. Scoop the shells onto individual serving plates. Serve hot.

Cook's Notes: *Never forage for wild mushrooms without proper knowledge of what is edible and what is poisonous; looks can be deceiving. When in doubt, go without—and substitute with any type of meaty mushroom from the market. If fontina cheese is too soft to grate, pop it in the freezer for a few minutes.*

Autumn Harvest Lasagna

This lasagna is layered with roasted butternut squash and orchard apples, sautéed kale and fresh sage. Everything is blanketed in a generous helping of indulgent "white sauce," also known as béchamel. If you come across a petite butternut squash, the ones that fit in the palm of your hand, one of them would work perfectly here. Otherwise, portion off a larger squash. Make sure to use heat-tolerant apples— I lean on the sweet-tartness of Honeycrisp or Gala apples, as they don't fall apart in the oven.

Serves 6

10 tbsp (150 g) butter, divided

8 oz (227 g) fontina cheese, grated

8 oz (227 g) mozzarella cheese, grated

½ lb (225 g) butternut squash, peeled, seeded and sliced lengthwise ¼ inch (6 mm) thick

1 Honeycrisp apple, peeled, cored and sliced ¼ inch (6 mm) thick

2 tbsp (30 ml) light, unrefined olive oil

Kosher salt and freshly ground pepper

2 tbsp (30 ml) extra-virgin olive oil

1 onion, thinly sliced

5 oz (142 g [about 1 small bunch]) kale, center stems removed, leaves roughly chopped

1 clove garlic, finely grated

¼ cup (60 ml) Sauvignon Blanc

9 lasagna noodles (no-boil type works well, too)

4 cups (1 L) whole milk

½ cup (62 g) unbleached, all-purpose flour

10 sage leaves

¼ tsp ground nutmeg

Preheat the oven to 425°F (220°C). Grease a 9 x 13-inch (23 x 33-cm) baking dish with 2 tablespoons (30 g) of butter and set aside. Mix the two cheeses together and refrigerate them until ready to use.

Line two baking sheets with parchment paper. On one, arrange the squash slices in a single layer. On the other, arrange the apple slices. Drizzle each sheet with 1 tablespoon (15 ml) of light, unrefined olive oil and massage onto the squash and apples. Season with salt and pepper. Place the apples on the top tier of the oven if possible, and roast until the squash and apples begin to soften and the edges are lightly crisp, about 15 minutes, keeping a watchful eye that the apples do not burn. Remove from the oven and set aside. Reduce the oven temperature to 350°F (175°C).

Add the extra-virgin olive oil to a 12-inch (30-cm) skillet over low-medium heat. When hot and shimmery, add the onion and lightly sprinkle with salt. Sauté, stirring often, until the onion is tender and caramelized, about 10 minutes. Add the kale and sauté until tender, about 5 minutes. Note that the kale should be done to your liking, as it will not soften much further in the oven and will only cook for a few minutes longer with the addition of the wine. Add the garlic and stir until fragrant, 30 seconds. Add the wine and cook until it has completely reduced, 3 to 5 minutes. Turn off the heat. Use a slotted spoon to transfer the kale mixture to a bowl. Season with salt and pepper, gently toss and set aside.

Meanwhile, bring a large pot of water to a boil. (If you are using no-boil noodles you can skip this step.)

Generously salt the water and add the lasagna. Cook until a few minutes shy of al dente, tender yet firm to the bite, according to the package directions. Drain and set aside in a single layer on parchment paper to cool.

In a small saucepan, heat the milk, taking care not to scorch. In another medium saucepan, melt 8 tablespoons (120 g) of butter over low heat. Add the flour to the butter, whisking constantly, to make a roux and to rid the mixture of any flour taste, about 1 minute. Slowly whisk in the warm milk and the sage leaves. Season to taste with salt and pepper. Raise the heat to moderate and bring the sauce to a low boil, continuing to whisk, then reduce to a simmer. Cook until the sauce becomes thick but still pourable, about 5 minutes. Remove the pan from the heat. Discard the sage leaves. Season with nutmeg and stir to combine.

(continued)

Autumn Harvest Lasagna (Continued)

To prepare the lasagna, halve the butternut squash, apples and kale mixture. Separate the combined grated cheese into three parts.

Add a full ladle of béchamel sauce evenly to the bottom of the buttered baking dish. Next add three lasagna noodles across, trying not to overlap. Top the noodles with another full ladle of béchamel sauce, using more sauce if necessary, to spread it out evenly. Add one-third of the cheese mixture in an even layer. Then, layer evenly with one half of the butternut squash and apple slices and the kale mixture. Drizzle the vegetables with a half ladle of béchamel sauce. Add three more noodles and repeat the layering again in the exact same way. For the top layer, add the last three noodles. Top with a full ladle of béchamel sauce, using more if necessary, over the noodles. Sprinkle the last of the cheese on top. Bake until the cheese is bubbling and beginning to brown in some spots, 30 to 35 minutes.

Let the lasagna stand at least 15 minutes, to properly set, before serving.

Pasta Giada alla Olive (Pasta with Olives)

This is one of my daughter Giada's favorite dishes and was therefore named for her. This recipe is reminiscent of a puttanesca sauce, in that it uses tomatoes, capers and olives—though I prefer a mix of varying types of olives and only roughly chop them. The irregular shape of the broken lasagna adds to the interest and the comfort of this dish. Get the kids involved with this recipe—they'll love breaking the noodles! A splash of red wine adds depth to the sauce and leaves its fragrance behind after it has cooked out. The only thing you'll have to keep in mind is that the olive ratio should be slightly less than the liquids you're using. The sauce should be fluid and loose and should not resemble a tapenade.

Serves 4–6

1 lb (454 g) lasagna noodles

Kosher salt

¼ cup (60 ml) extra-virgin olive oil, plus more for drizzling

¼ tsp Aleppo pepper (substitute with red pepper flakes)

1 small onion, diced

4 tbsp (56 g) tomato paste

1 large clove garlic, finely grated

½ cup (120 ml) dry red wine

1 (28-oz [794-g]) can San Marzano whole peeled tomatoes (including the juice), ends trimmed

1 tbsp (9 g) capers, rinsed and drained

1 cup (180 g) mixed olives, pitted and roughly chopped (Italian Castelvetrano, Greek Kalamata and black oil-cured)

Grated Parmigiano–Reggiano or local cheese with a hard and sharp profile, to garnish

Break the lasagna noodles into irregular bite-sized pieces over a large bowl and set aside.

Bring a large pot of water to a boil, generously salt and then add the broken lasagna noodles. Continuously stir the pasta for the first 15 to 20 seconds as the flat shape of the broken noodles will try hard to suction together. Cook the pasta until just shy of al dente, tender yet firm to the bite, according to the package directions. Reserve ½ cup (120 ml) of the pasta water before draining. Drain well.

In the meantime, to a large 12-inch (30-cm) skillet with deep sides over low-medium heat, add the olive oil. When it is hot and shimmery, add the Aleppo pepper (or red pepper flakes) and onion. Sprinkle lightly with salt and sauté, stirring often, until the onion is tender and translucent and has begun to caramelize, about 10 minutes, careful not to let the oil smoke.

Push the onions to the sides of the pan to expose the hot center of the pan. Add the tomato paste to the center, spreading it out a bit with the back of a cooking spoon, and let it sit until it begins to caramelize, 2 to 3 minutes. Stir the onions and the tomato paste together to incorporate. Add the garlic and stir until fragrant, about 30 seconds.

Remove the pan from the heat and carefully add the wine. Return to low-medium heat and scrape the bottom of the skillet to deglaze any flavorful brown bits that may have accumulated. Add the tomatoes along with the juices and use a square-head potato masher or the back of a wooden spoon to roughly break and crush the tomatoes, stirring well to mix. Add the capers and olives, stirring again. Continue to simmer, stirring often, 10 minutes. If the pasta is not finished cooking, it's fine to turn off the heat under the olive mixture at this point.

Add the pasta and ¼ cup (60 ml) of the reserved pasta water; toss until the flavors are well incorporated, 1 minute. If necessary, add a splash more of the reserved pasta water to loosen the pasta. The sauce should be silky and not sticky or pasty. Serve with grated cheese and a generous drizzle of extra-virgin olive oil.

Spaghetti and Kale Pangrattato

Pangrattato simply means flavored, crispy, grated breadcrumbs that have been toasted, historically referred to as the "poor-man's" Parmesan cheese. Like many dishes with humble beginnings, the ingredients in this dish are simple, but the taste is memorable. The anchovies almost completely disintegrate in the hot oil, leaving behind an essence that is perfectly salty. Food experts have called this flavor "umami," a difficult-to-describe fifth taste that goes beyond salty, sweet, sour or bitter and can only be explained as a savory taste that lingers, making you crave more.

Serves 4–6

1 cup (100 g) fresh coarse breadcrumbs, preferably from the heels of few-days-old ciabatta bread or substitute with quality store-bought

¼ cup (60 ml) plus ¼ cup (60 ml) extra-virgin olive oil, divided, plus more for drizzling

¼ tsp red pepper flakes

6 anchovy fillets

Kosher salt

1 lb (454 g) spaghetti

3 medium cloves garlic, thinly sliced

2-3 oz (60-90 g) kale leaves, roughly chopped, center stems removed

Freshly ground pepper, to taste

In a high-powered food processor, pulse the bread to create coarse breadcrumbs. Set aside. Skip this step if using store-bought breadcrumbs.

In a large 12-inch (30-cm) skillet, add ¼ cup (60 ml) of olive oil over low–medium heat. Add the red pepper flakes and cook until toasted, about 1 minute. Add the anchovies to the pan, breaking them up with a wooden spoon until they dissolve, about 3 minutes. Raise the heat to medium and add the breadcrumbs, stirring constantly, until they are deeply golden brown, about 5 minutes (don't be afraid to let them darken, just take care not to let them burn). Remove the skillet from the heat. Taste and salt only if necessary, since anchovies are naturally salty. Spoon the breadcrumb mixture into a medium bowl and set aside. When the skillet is cool, wipe it clean with a paper towel and reserve it for later.

Bring a large pot of water to a boil. Generously salt the water and add the spaghetti. Cook until about 1 minute shy of al dente, tender yet firm to the bite, according to the package directions. Reserve 2 cups (480 ml) of the pasta water before draining. Drain well.

Meanwhile, into the reserved skillet add ¼ cup (60 ml) of olive oil over low–medium heat. When the oil is hot and shimmery, add the garlic, stirring until golden, about 4 minutes, taking care not to burn. Add the kale and sauté until tender and bright green, about 2 minutes. Season lightly with salt and pepper.

Add 1 cup (240 ml) of the reserved pasta water to the skillet. Raise the heat to medium and season lightly with salt. Allow the contents to come to a low boil.

Add the spaghetti, tossing to coat, about 1 to 2 minutes, noting that it will look very watery at first. When most of the water has been absorbed, add the remaining 1 cup (240 ml) of reserved water, season lightly again with salt and toss until most but not all the water has been absorbed, 1 to 2 minutes. Turn off the heat.

Add less than half of the breadcrumb mixture to the pasta and toss to mix. Drizzle with olive oil and freshly ground pepper. Serve immediately. Sprinkle breadcrumbs on top of each serving and pass the rest at the table.

Rigatoni with Radicchio and Warm Gorgonzola

This is a grown-up version of mac and cheese. The unexpected combination of seasonal radicchio and pasta paired with the savory saltiness of warm Gorgonzola makes this an indulgent autumn comfort dish. I love this meal best when served in a warm bowl, cupped in my hands and pulled close to my chest with a glass of my favorite red wine at hand.

Serves 4

2 tbsp (10 g) fine Italian-seasoned breadcrumbs

2 tbsp (10 g) grated Parmigiano-Reggiano cheese

¼ cup (60 ml) plus 1 tbsp (15 ml) extra-virgin olive oil, divided

1 medium onion, halved and sliced thin

Kosher salt, as needed

2 small heads radicchio (about ¾ lb [340 g]), quartered, cored and sliced thin

1 small clove garlic, finely grated

Freshly ground pepper, to taste

12 oz (340 g) rigatoni

2 cups (480 ml) whole milk

4 tbsp (60 g) butter

¼ cup (31 g) unbleached, all-purpose flour

4 oz (112 g) crumbled Gorgonzola cheese

Mix the breadcrumbs and Parmigiano cheese together. Add 1 tablespoon (15 ml) of the olive oil and stir, pressing the mixture into the oil. Continue stirring and pressing until the mixture resembles coarse, wet sand. Set aside.

In a large 12-inch (30-cm) oven-safe skillet over high heat, add ¼ cup (60 ml) of the olive oil. When it is hot and shimmery, add the onion and sprinkle lightly with salt. Sauté until tender and caramelized, about 10 minutes.

Add the radicchio. Sauté, stirring often, until the radicchio is tender and has cooked down significantly, 5 to 6 minutes. Add the garlic and stir until fragrant, 30 seconds. Season with salt and pepper to taste. Set the skillet aside.

In the meantime, bring a large pot of water to a boil. Generously salt the water and add the pasta. Cook until about 1 minute shy of al dente, tender yet firm to the bite, according to the package directions. Reserve ½ cup (120 ml) of the pasta water before draining. Drain well.

Add the milk to a small saucepan over low-medium heat. Being careful not to scorch, stir the milk until it is warmed through.

In another small saucepan, warm the butter over low-medium heat. When the butter is melted, add the flour to the butter and whisk continuously until the flour turns golden brown, 2 to 3 minutes. Carefully add the warm milk to the roux and simmer until the mixture thickens into a sauce, 2 minutes. Turn off the heat and season to taste with salt and pepper.

Add the pasta and ¼ cup (60 ml) of the reserved pasta water to the skillet with the radicchio, tossing well to combine. Pour the sauce over the pasta, giving a gentle toss to coat evenly. Add the Gorgonzola and stir again—the heat from the pasta will warm and melt the Gorgonzola. Taste and adjust the seasonings if necessary. Top with the breadcrumb mixture, then drizzle sparingly with olive oil.

Place the skillet under a broiler set on high until the breadcrumbs are toasted, 3 to 5 minutes. Broilers vary, so keep a watchful eye. Serve hot.

Broken Lasagna with White Truffle Butter and Fried Sage

Autumn is truffle season! Though one might not always have access to truffles, you can still wow your friends and family with indulgent truffle butter. You can find it in the specialty section of many markets or online from a reputable retailer. With gorgeous specks of white truffles in the butter, a splash of heavy cream and a handful of fresh sage, you might literally want to lick the plate clean. I like to use broken lasagna noodles for this dish because their wide body makes it easy to mop up all that delectable sauce. Enjoy this dish alone or alongside your favorite main course.

Serves 4–6

1 tsp kosher salt, plus more for cooking the pasta

1 lb (454 g) lasagna noodles, broken into large bite-sized pieces

6 tbsp (90 g) white truffle butter

10 fresh sage leaves

½ cup (120 ml) heavy cream

Freshly ground pepper, to taste

Grated Parmigiano-Reggiano or local cheese with a hard and sharp profile, to garnish

Bring a large pot of water to a boil. Generously salt the water and add the pasta, cooking until almost al dente, tender yet firm to the bite, according to the package directions. Reserve 1 cup (240 ml) of the pasta water before draining. Drain well.

About 5 minutes before the pasta has finished cooking, begin to prepare the truffle butter sauce.

In a large 12-inch (30-cm) skillet over low–medium heat, heat the truffle butter until it just begins to foam. Add the sage leaves, being careful when you add them as sage leaves tend to pop a bit while they're cooking (and even more so if they are damp, so make sure they are dry). Let the sage sit undisturbed to begin to crisp well, about 2 minutes. Using a slotted spoon or a pair of tongs, remove the sage from the skillet and set aside on a paper towel–lined plate.

Lower the heat and slowly add the cream, 1 teaspoon of salt and a few turns of freshly ground pepper. Stir to mix well and bring the cream to a simmer, about 1 minute.

Turn off the heat. Add the pasta and ½ cup (120 ml) of the reserved pasta water, tossing to coat well. Pasta should be silky, not pasty. If needed, use more of the reserved pasta water, a little at a time, to help loosen the pasta. To serve, garnish with freshly grated cheese and fried sage leaves (whole or crumbled). The sauce will continue to thicken upon standing.

Orecchiette with Caramelized Brussels Sprouts and Toasted Hazelnut Oil

Ever since I roasted Brussels sprouts on their stalk and shared the recipe on my blog, I've been looking for other ways to enjoy these little cabbages. Here they are sliced into thin ribbons, like confetti, and caramelized. A splash of vegetable broth gives the dish some fluidity, and it's all enhanced with toasted hazelnut oil and a subtle kick of heat from red pepper flakes.

Serves 4–6

1 lb (454 g) Brussels sprouts

½ cup (120 ml) extra-virgin olive oil, divided, plus more for drizzling

4 tbsp (60 g) butter, divided

⅓ cup (40 g) coarsely chopped hazelnuts (consistency should be like coarse sand, not fine and powdery)

Kosher salt and freshly ground pepper, to taste

1 lb (454 g) orecchiette

2 shallots, thinly sliced

¼ tsp crushed red pepper flakes

2 cloves garlic, finely grated

1 cup (240 ml) vegetable broth

Grated Parmigiano–Reggiano or local cheese with a hard and sharp profile, to garnish

Prepare the Brussels sprouts by cutting the sprouts in half and slicing them thin. Rinse, drain and set aside.

Prepare the hazelnuts by heating ¼ cup (60 ml) of the olive oil and 2 tablespoons (30 g) of butter in a medium skillet over medium heat. When the oil is hot and the butter is melted, add the hazelnuts and toast until golden, 3 to 5 minutes. Season lightly with salt and pepper and set aside.

Bring a large pot of water to a boil. Generously salt the water, then add the pasta. Cook the pasta until just shy of al dente, tender yet firm to the bite, according to the package directions. Reserve ½ cup (120 ml) of the pasta water before draining. Drain well.

In the meantime, in a large 12-inch (30-cm) skillet with deep sides, heat the remaining ¼ cup (60 ml) of the olive oil and 2 tablespoons (30 g) of butter over medium-high heat. When the oil is hot and shimmery and the butter is melted, add the shallots and Brussels sprouts. Season with salt and pepper. Stir well to coat the sprouts and let them sit, stirring often, until they are caramelized and tender, 15 to 20 minutes. Add the red pepper flakes and garlic and sauté until the garlic is fragrant, 30 seconds.

Add the vegetable broth. Scrape the bottom of the skillet to deglaze any flavorful brown bits that may have accumulated. It's fine to turn off the heat at this point if the pasta is not ready.

Add the pasta and turn the heat to a simmer. Add ¼ cup (60 ml) of the reserved pasta water and stir to combine until most of the liquid has been absorbed, 1 minute. Taste and adjust the seasonings.

Add the toasted hazelnuts and the hazelnut oil and toss to combine, being sure to scoop from the bottom and fold, until most of the oil has been absorbed and the pasta has finished cooking, about 1 minute more. If necessary, use the rest of the reserved pasta water to loosen the pasta.

To serve, divide into individual serving bowls and garnish with grated cheese.

Butternut Squash Pasta Bake with Whole Cranberries and Brie

It's that time of the year when whole fresh cranberries are available by the bagful. This baked penne recipe tastes like the holidays when sausage, kale and butternut squash come together to make a full-flavored dish. Red wine accents the cranberry sauce used in this recipe; however, feel free to swap it out to make use of the cranberry sauce that is left over from your holiday table.

Serves 6

1 cup (100 g) whole fresh cranberries

2 tbsp (25 g) light brown sugar

½ cup (120 ml) dry red wine

2 tbsp (30 g) butter

Kosher salt and freshly ground pepper, to taste

2 tbsp (30 ml) extra-virgin olive oil, divided

1 onion, finely diced

1 lb (454 g) sausage, casings removed

3 medium cloves garlic, finely grated

1½ cups (360 ml) vegetable stock

2 cups (280 g) cubed butternut or kabocha squash, cut into about 1-inch (2.5-cm)-sized pieces

2 cups (135 g) chopped kale (substitute with Swiss chard)

1 lb (454 g) penne

⅔ cup (160 ml) half and half

½ cup (50 g) finely grated Parmigiano–Reggiano

1½ cups (168 g) mozzarella, shredded

8 oz (227 g) Brie (skin removed), cubed

Preheat the oven to 350°F (175°C).

In a medium saucepan over medium heat, combine the cranberries, brown sugar, red wine and butter. Season lightly with salt and pepper and cook, stirring frequently, until the cranberries soften and burst, and the mixture thickens, 10 to 15 minutes. The consistency should be just thick enough to spread without being runny. Set aside.

Add the olive oil to a large 13- to 15-inch (33- to 38-cm) oven-safe skillet over low-medium heat. When the oil is hot and shimmery, add the onion and sausage. Cook, breaking up the sausage into small, bite-sized pieces, until browned and the onion is tender, 10 minutes. Add the garlic and stir until fragrant, 30 seconds. Add the stock and scrape the bottom of the pan to deglaze any flavorful brown bits that may have accumulated. Add the squash and kale, and season to taste with salt and pepper. Stir well to coat. Cover, cook on low–medium heat, stirring often, until the squash is tender and soft, 15 to 20 minutes.

In the meantime, bring a large pot of water to a boil. Generously salt the water, then add the pasta. Cook until about 2 to 3 minutes shy of al dente, tender yet firm to the bite, according to the package directions. Reserve ¼ cup (60 ml) of the pasta water before draining. Drain well.

Add the half and half and Parmigiano to the skillet, and turn off the heat. Gently stir. Add the pasta and the reserved pasta water, tossing well to coat. Randomly dollop the top with the cranberry sauce, using the back of a spoon to lightly spread it out, noting that it isn't supposed to cover the dish evenly.

Top with the mozzarella and Brie, sprinkling the cheese on any bare spots between the cranberry sauce first. Tent with foil and cook in the preheated oven until the cheese is bubbling, about 30 minutes. Remove the foil and place the skillet under a broiler set to high. Broil until the cheese turns golden, 3 to 5 minutes, keeping a watchful eye as broiler temperatures vary. Allow the contents to set for 5 minutes before serving.

Pasta Foriana (Sweet and Savory Nut and Raisin Sauce)

Foriana sauce is native to the island of Ischia off the coast of Naples, where it is served on pasta as a Lenten dish, though I enjoy it once autumn arrives, mostly because the colors of the golden raisins and currants look like the changing seasons in a bowl. The raisins and currants steep in boiling water to soften and plump. Then they are tossed with long strands of your favorite pasta, garlic, pine nuts and grated cheese for a creamy sauce that comes together in the time it takes to boil pasta.

Serves 4–6

½ cup (80 g) golden raisins

½ cup (80 g) Zante currants

¼ cup (30 g) pine nuts

2 cloves garlic, smashed

Kosher salt, to taste

1 lb (454 g) linguine (or other long pasta of choice)

¼ cup (60 ml) extra-virgin olive oil, plus more for drizzling

3 tbsp (45 g) butter

Freshly ground pepper, to taste

Grated Parmigiano–Reggiano or local cheese with a hard and sharp profile, to garnish

Place the raisins and currants in a medium heat-safe bowl. Pour boiling water over them until they are fully submerged. Gently stir to make sure they are not sticking together. Steep for 15 minutes, then drain well and set aside. This process will soften the raisins and currants and plump them up. While they steep, prepare the other ingredients.

In a food processor, briefly pulse the pine nuts and garlic just until they are coarsely crumbled, keeping in mind that overprocessing will result in a sandy paste and will make the dish far too thick. Set aside.

Bring a large pot of water to a boil. Generously salt and then add the pasta. Cook until just shy of al dente, tender yet firm to the bite, according to the package directions. Reserve 1 cup (240 ml) of the pasta water before draining. Drain well.

Add the olive oil and butter to a large 12-inch (30-cm) skillet over low heat. When the oil is hot and the butter is melted, carefully add ½ cup (120 ml) of the reserved pasta water and the pasta to the skillet, giving it a toss. Add the pine nut mixture along with the raisins and currants, and toss again to combine. Turn off the heat and add the rest of the reserved pasta water, continuing to toss until most, but not all, of the water is absorbed, 1 to 2 minutes. The consistency should be silky, not sticky.

To serve, season with freshly ground pepper, a generous drizzle of olive oil and freshly grated cheese.

Fresh Sage Fettuccine with Brown Butter

When fresh sage overflows in terra cotta pots outside of my kitchen door, I'll look for any way to snip those fragrant leaves. When roughly chopped, fresh sage releases its woodsy perfume, flavoring fresh pasta and dotting long strands of fettuccine with specks of its gentle green hue. A simple sauce of brown butter and pasta water is all that is required to complete this dish. A few turns of freshly cracked pepper and freshly grated cheese is the perfect garnish.

Serves 4–6

⅓ cup (10 g) finely chopped fresh sage

Basic Pasta Dough (page 16)

8 tbsp (120 g) butter

Kosher salt, to taste

Freshly ground pepper, to taste

Grated Parmigiano-Reggiano or local cheese with a hard and sharp profile, to garnish

To prepare the fresh pasta, add the chopped fresh sage to the egg mixture in the Basic Pasta Dough recipe (page 16), then continue with the rest of the directions for kneading, rolling out and cutting the dough.

When the pasta is cut into fettuccine and drying, bring a large pot of water to a boil.

Meanwhile, melt the butter in a large 12-inch (30-cm) stainless-steel skillet (a light-colored pan will help you to see when the butter is browning) over low–medium heat. Cook, stirring constantly, until the butter begins to foam and brown flecks appear. Keep stirring until the butter is about one shade lighter than you'd like it to be. Turn off the heat and continue to stir. The butter will continue to darken and take on a deeply nutty aroma.

Generously salt the boiling water and add the pasta. Note that fresh pasta will cook faster, usually within 1 to 2 minutes, so keep a watchful eye. Before draining, reserve 1 cup (240 ml) of the pasta water. Drain well.

Add the pasta and ½ cup (120 ml) of the pasta water to the skillet with the brown butter. Toss until the water is mostly absorbed. If more moisture is needed, add more reserved pasta water, a little at a time, and continue to toss until the desired consistency is reached. Pasta should be silky and buttery.

To serve, top with freshly ground pepper and grated cheese.

Fresh Pumpkin Pappardelle with Browned Rosemary Butter

Pumpkin, the king of the autumn harvest, has an honorary stay in my kitchen from late September through November. Pumpkins add a rustic charm to my family table and are a reliable ingredient in my autumn cooking. This dish uses pure pumpkin puree (either fresh or canned) to add a subtle hint of flavor and an earthy autumnal color. I've decided to update a blog recipe favorite by forgoing the pasta machine and rolling the dough out by hand. Fresh rosemary enhances butter that has been browned, taking on a nutty caramel hue and taste.

Serves 4–6

¼ cup (60 g) pure pumpkin puree (homemade or canned)

Basic Pasta Dough (page 16)

½ cup (115 g) butter

2 sprigs fresh rosemary

Kosher salt, to taste

⅓ cup (60 g) Pecorino cheese, plus more to garnish

Freshly ground pepper, to taste

To prepare the fresh pasta, add the pumpkin puree to the egg mixture in the Basic Pasta Dough recipe (page 16) and continue to follow the instructions there for kneading the dough and letting it rest.

After the dough has rested, knead it a few more times. Cut it into four even pieces, working with one piece at a time and covering the rest as needed. Lightly dust a rolling pin with flour and begin to roll the dough out on a lightly floured work surface until it is paper thin, or just a tad meatier if you'd like a more full-bodied noodle. Using a sharp knife or a pizza cutter, cut the dough into approximately 1-inch (2.5-cm)-wide strips.

In a single layer, lay the noodles out on a large cotton towel or sheet. Very lightly dust the noodles with flour and allow them time to dry for 30 minutes. You can feel when they begin to dry as they become firmer to the touch. When they are almost dry, bring a large pot of water to a boil.

Meanwhile, melt the butter in a large 12-inch (30-cm) stainless-steel skillet (a light-colored pan will help you to see when the butter is browning) over low–medium heat. Add the rosemary sprigs. Cook, stirring constantly, until the butter begins to foam and brown flecks appear. Keep stirring until the butter is about one shade lighter than you'd like it to be. Turn off the heat and continue to stir. The butter will continue to darken and take on a deep nutty caramel aroma. Remove and discard the rosemary sprigs.

Generously salt the boiling water and add the fresh pasta. Note that fresh pasta cooks much faster than dried, usually in 1 to 2 minutes. Reserve 2 cups (480 ml) of the pasta water before draining. Drain well.

Working quickly, add 1 cup (120 ml) of the reserved pasta water to the skillet with the butter. Add the pasta and slowly sprinkle in the Pecorino cheese, while whisking quickly, and continue to toss until most of the liquid is absorbed, 1 minute. Season with freshly ground pepper and toss again. Add the remaining pasta water, ¼ cup (60 ml) at a time as needed, to loosen the pasta. The consistency should be silky and buttery.

To serve, divide onto individual plates and top with freshly ground pepper and grated cheese.

Fresh Potato Gnocchi with Creamy Pumpkin Sauce

This recipe uses fresh potato gnocchi and pairs it with a creamy pumpkin sauce and the warm notes of nutmeg. The sauce will yield extra, or just the right amount, depending on the moisture in the gnocchi; therefore, it is best to ladle the sauce as desired, as opposed to adding it all at once to the gnocchi. While potato gnocchi is more accurately a dumpling, it is very much considered a type of potato pasta and is usually found amongst traditional pastas in supermarkets and on restaurant menus. It is not difficult to make at all, though using your judgment is as important as using the right ingredients. Making gnocchi, like fresh pasta, relies on feel and touch. This dish stands well on its own or as an accompaniment to roasted chicken for a more substantial meal.

Serves 2–4

Gnocchi

4 medium russet potatoes, scrubbed

1½ cups (187 g) unbleached all-purpose flour, plus more for kneading and rolling

1 tsp kosher salt

1 egg yolk, lightly beaten

Preheat the oven to 375°F (190°C). Line two baking sheets with wax paper and set aside for flouring the gnocchi.

Pierce the potatoes several times with a fork to allow moisture to escape. Place the whole potatoes on a rimmed baking sheet and bake until very tender and easily pierced with a knife, 1 to 1½ hours. After they are cooked, slice the tops of the potatoes lengthwise to let out the steam. Once cool enough to handle, spoon out the potato from the skins. Discard the skins.

Use a potato ricer or the medium-sized holes on a food mill to pass the potatoes through in small batches and into a large bowl. Allow the potatoes to cool almost completely.

Lightly flour a work surface. In a small bowl, mix the flour and salt together. Add the egg to the potatoes and mix well with a fork. Add the flour and salt mixture to the potatoes and begin to mix by hand. The mixture will feel clumpy and sticky. Continue to press down and mix until the mixture comes together. Place the mass of dough onto the floured work surface and wash hands clean, then dry them well.

Knead the dough until all the flour is well incorporated, 1 to 2 minutes. The dough should be smooth and soft and only a little sticky. If too sticky, dust with more flour—you'll know it's too sticky when remnants of dough continue to pull away from the mound and stick to your hands instead. On a floured surface, cut the dough into four equal pieces, or into smaller pieces if that's easier. Working with one section at a time, roll the dough between your fingers and the work surface into a long ¾-inch (2-cm)-thick strip. Cut the strip into ¾-inch (2-cm) pieces.

Leave the cut pieces as-is, or make an indent with your thumb in the center, or roll each piece against the tines of a fork. Transfer to the wax-paper–lined baking sheets and dust with flour.

If using within the next hour or two, it is fine to leave the gnocchi on the baking sheets. If making the gnocchi ahead, freeze them. The uncooked gnocchi pieces can be frozen on the baking sheets, then transferred to a resealable plastic bag and kept in the freezer for up to 1 month. Boil frozen gnocchi without defrosting.

Pumpkin Sauce

3 tbsp (45 ml) extra-virgin olive oil, divided, plus more as needed

5 sage leaves

1 shallot, thinly sliced

Kosher salt, to taste

2 tbsp (30 g) butter

2 tbsp (16 g) cornstarch

⅔ cup (160 ml) milk

Freshly ground pepper, to taste

¼ tsp ground nutmeg

1 cup (245 g) pumpkin puree (fresh or substitute with pure canned pumpkin)

1½ cups (360 ml) vegetable broth

1 lb (454 g) fresh gnocchi

Grated Parmigiano-Reggiano or local cheese with a hard and sharp profile, to garnish

Bring a large pot of water to a boil.

To fry the sage leaves for the garnish, add 1 tablespoon (15 ml) of olive oil to a small skillet. When the oil is hot, add the sage leaves and fry until crispy, about 1 minute. Transfer to a paper towel-lined plate to absorb the excess oil. Set aside.

In the meantime, in a large 12-inch (30-cm) skillet, heat 2 tablespoons (30 ml) of olive oil over low-medium heat. When the oil is hot and shimmery, add the shallot, sprinkle lightly with salt and cook until the shallot is tender and beginning to caramelize, about 10 minutes.

Add the butter to the skillet and when melted, add the cornstarch, whisking continuously to avoid lumps and until well incorporated. Add the milk, salt, pepper and nutmeg, and continue to whisk until well blended.

Add the pumpkin puree and broth, stirring well to mix. Simmer the sauce for 5 to 10 minutes. The sauce should be loose and creamy, not thick like a puree. Turn off the heat.

Generously salt the boiling water and add the gnocchi. Fresh gnocchi will cook fast, usually in 2 to 4 minutes, and are done when they rise to the surface of the water. Reserve 1 cup (240 ml) of the pasta water before draining. Drain well.

To serve, transfer the gnocchi to a serving bowl, add a scant ¼ cup (60 ml) of the reserved pasta water and the desired amount of sauce. Toss well to mix. Pass the remaining sauce at the table. Garnish with the grated cheese and fried sage (crumbled or whole).

*See photo on page 18.

Cook's Notes: *The amount of flour needed will vary depending on the moisture level of the potatoes. Use your judgment as you go. To aid in drying out the potatoes, the best method is to bake the potatoes in an oven, not the microwave, and do not boil.*

> *"Winter is the time for comfort, for good food and*
> *warmth, for the touch of a friendly hand and for*
> *a talk beside the fire: it is the time for home."*
>
> —Edith Sitwell

WINTER

The farm markets that opened with the slow rise of the sun have mostly closed their doors for the winter. The fields that bustled with locals and out-of-towners alike, picking apples and pumpkins, lie in a quiet slumber. Now we rely on our farmer friends from warmer climates to share the fruits of their labor, quite literally, as citrus fruits are at the height of their season. Caramelizing citrus in olive oil, like in Ravioli with Caramelized Blood Oranges and Escarole (page 68), adds a bright note to these long, cold days. Citrus complements pasta beautifully, especially when paired with a delicate winter green, like escarole, with its tenderness aiding in our anticipation for those delicate spring days ahead.

Pears are also at the height of their season, and they are not to be overlooked in savory dishes, either. The maple trees around here are ripe for tapping, and I've incorporated both into a pasta dish that is unexpected and often requested. It is the contrasting bite of a sharp cheese that balances out the sweetness, making Pasta with Maple-Caramelized Pears and Gorgonzola (page 67) a delectable seasonal dish.

If I had to choose what I love most about winter cooking, it would be the techniques: long simmers, braising and toasting. Did you know that you can toast plain white pasta? Toasting creates a wonderful nutty profile for the pasta; it changes the texture and the color. I like to pair toasted pasta with a simple oil and garlic sauce to showcase, and not compete with, the beautiful color of the pasta, such as in Toasted Spaghetti Aglio e Olio (page 63).

There are unique spices, too, that aid in the warmth that winter beckons. Have you ever considered cooking with cocoa? Take a peek at Rigatoni with Dark Cocoa and Red Wine Short Rib Ragu (page 87). Natural cocoa is quite bitter on its own and is rightfully considered a spice. It has been used for centuries by Italians to enhance savory dishes like risotto, polenta, meat and pasta dishes—not just for sweets and baking.

Time at the stove welcomes us more in the winter than any other season with its cozy heat and soul-satisfying aromas, warming us up from the inside out.

Toasted Spaghetti Aglio e Olio

Have you ever toasted pasta? Just a few minutes in the oven and you'll completely transform plain white pasta into a rich, tawny-colored and nutty-tasting version of itself. I love toasting pasta in the winter; it adds an earthy layer of flavor to a very simple sauce of garlic (aglio) and oil (olio) (pronounced ah-lee-oh oh-lee-oh; it's fun to say!). In my house this dish is lovingly referred to as Pasta "Alleluia!"—it was how my mother pronounced it as a child, and out of sheer amusement my grandmother called it that too, and so it remained for the next three generations.

Serves 4–6

1 lb (454 g) spaghetti

Kosher salt

½ cup (120 ml) extra-virgin olive oil, plus more for drizzling

3 large cloves garlic, thinly sliced

Freshly ground black pepper, to taste

Crushed red pepper, to garnish

Pecorino cheese, to garnish

Preheat the oven to 350°F (175°C). Line a rimmed baking sheet with parchment paper. Spread the dry pasta out evenly on the baking sheet. Bake for 6 to 9 minutes for 1 pound (454 g) of pasta, a little less time for a smaller portion, moving the pasta around occasionally to make sure it toasts evenly and baking until the pasta is golden brown and has a toasted aroma. Set aside.

Bring a large pot of water to a boil. Generously salt the water and add the pasta. Cook until al dente, tender yet firm to the bite, according to the package directions—noting that toasted pasta will always have an al dente texture, so use the package directions as a guideline. The best way to know if it is done will be to taste it, using your judgment and preference. Reserve 2 cups (480 ml) of the pasta water before draining. Drain well.

Meanwhile, heat the olive oil in a large 12-inch (30-cm) skillet with deep sides over medium heat. Add the garlic and sauté, stirring occasionally, until lightly golden brown, about 3 minutes, taking care not to let it burn. Season generously with coarsely ground black pepper.

Add 1 cup (240 ml) of the pasta water to the pan. Add the pasta and cook, tossing and adding more pasta water only if needed, a little at a time, until sauce lightly coats the pasta, about 2 minutes.

Serve garnished with the desired amount of red pepper flakes and coarsely ground black pepper, grated pecorino and an extra drizzle of olive oil.

White Wine Linguine

I first had pasta cooked in red wine in Tuscany (see my autumn Red Wine Spaghetti with Swiss Chard [page 25]). Inspired by that recipe, I've created a white wine version. In this dish an entire bottle of Sauvignon Blanc is used to finish cooking the pasta. No need to splurge on an expensive bottle. A modest price point wine will do, so long as it is a brand you enjoy, as the flavor and notes will be highlighted. The wine is absorbed, creating both a fragrant and full-flavored pasta, as well as doubling as a light sauce when combined with a splash of chicken broth and Parmigiano–Reggiano. The key here is to work simultaneously with two skillets to keep the heat consistent after the initial parboil.

Serves 4–6

Kosher salt, to taste

1 lb (454 g) linguine (or any other long pasta)

¼ cup (60 ml) extra-virgin olive oil, plus more for drizzling

1 clove garlic, smashed and thinly sliced

1 (25-oz [740-ml]) bottle Sauvignon Blanc

1 cup (240 ml) chicken broth

Freshly ground pepper

¼ cup (25 g) finely grated Parmigiano–Reggiano or local cheese with a hard and sharp profile, plus more to garnish

1 tbsp (15 g) butter

You'll need a stockpot and a 12-inch (30-cm) skillet with deep sides. We'll be working with both at the same time.

Bring a large pot of water to a boil. Generously salt and add the pasta. Boil until the pasta can fully bend while still undercooked, about 5 to 6 minutes. Reserve 2 cups (480 ml) of the pasta water before draining. Drain well.

Meanwhile, heat the olive oil in the skillet over low–medium heat. When hot and shimmery, add the garlic, stirring often until golden, about 3 minutes, taking care not to burn the garlic or it will taste bitter. Remove the skillet from the heat to carefully add the bottle of white wine, which may splatter at first. Add the broth and raise the heat to medium–high to bring the contents to a boil.

Add the parboiled pasta to the skillet and ½ cup (120 ml) of the reserved pasta water. Season with salt and freshly ground pepper. Keep the mixture at a boil and use tongs to toss frequently to prevent sticking.

Cook until the pasta is al dente, tender yet firm to the bite, and the liquid has been largely absorbed, though not entirely, tossing frequently, about 10 minutes. Add a little more of the reserved pasta water if the pasta absorbs too much. Keep a watchful eye as cooking times will differ depending on the type and brand of pasta.

While continuously tossing, add the grated cheese, a little at a time. By adding small amounts and tossing, the cheese will melt more evenly and will not stick to the bottom of the pan. Again, use more of the reserved pasta water, if necessary. Toss well. The pasta should be loose and silky and will continue to thicken upon standing.

Turn off the heat and add the butter, gently tossing to create a silky glaze. Taste and adjust the seasonings, if necessary.

To serve, drizzle lightly with olive oil, a few turns of freshly ground pepper and more grated cheese. Serve immediately.

Pasta with Maple-Caramelized Pears and Gorgonzola

Voluptuous pears, with their subtle sugary grain and light, watery-sweet nectar pair beautifully with the bite of creamy Gorgonzola—the two are commonly found together in many Italian dishes, as the cheese balances the sweet with just the right amount of salty. Local maple syrup adds a warm and comforting note while softened, plumped-up cranberries finish the dish as a vibrant ruby-colored garnish. Enjoy as-is or alongside roasted pork or chicken.

Serves 4–6

¼ cup (40 g) dried cranberries

Kosher salt

1 lb (454 g) rigatoni

4 tbsp (60 g) butter

3 tbsp (45 ml) pure maple syrup

4 Bosc pears, peeled, cored and sliced into ¼-inch (6-mm)–thick slices

1 cup (240 ml) chicken broth

4 oz (112 g) crumbled Gorgonzola cheese, plus more to garnish

Freshly ground pepper, to taste

To begin, place the cranberries in a heat-proof bowl and cover with enough boiling water to keep them submerged. Let the cranberries sit for 20 minutes to soften and plump. Drain and discard the water. Set the cranberries aside.

Bring a large pot of water to a boil. Generously salt the water and add the pasta. Cook until just shy of al dente, tender yet firm to the bite, according to the package directions. Reserve ½ cup (120 ml) of the pasta water before draining. Drain well.

In the meantime, melt the butter and maple syrup in a large 12-inch (30-cm) skillet over medium heat. Add the pears and give a gentle stir to coat them. Cook until the pears are tender and beginning to lightly caramelize, about 12 to 15 minutes. Use a slotted spoon to transfer the pears to a separate plate and set aside, leaving behind as much butter and maple in the skillet as possible.

Add the broth to the skillet and scrape the bottom of the pan to deglaze any flavorful brown bits that may have accumulated. Add the Gorgonzola and simmer, whisking until the cheese melts and the sauce reduces slightly, about 5 minutes.

Add the pasta and ¼ cup (60 ml) of the reserved pasta water to the skillet. Toss over low heat, 1 minute. Season lightly with freshly ground pepper. Add the remaining pasta water, a tablespoon (15 ml) at a time, if needed to loosen the pasta. Texture should be creamy and fluid, not pasty.

To serve, divide into individual portions and garnish with the cranberries, caramelized pears and additional Gorgonzola.

Ravioli with Caramelized Blood Oranges and Escarole

It's winter and citrus fruits are at the height of their season. For me, there's something summery about citrus, and that's just the brightness I crave when the dark of winter is long. Use organic oranges because we'll be roasting with the peels on. The aromatic juice from the caramelized orange slices will infuse the olive oil, and the peppery escarole will balance the dish perfectly. Ravioli pairs beautifully because of its two-part component of dough and filling—the essence from the citrus clings to the dough in a silky glaze, and when the ravioli is gently cut, the ricotta seeps out just enough to mingle with the fragrant oil. A fresh squeeze of juice at the end brings it all together.

Serves 4–6

3 organic blood oranges

Kosher salt, to taste

1 lb (454 g) ravioli (traditional cheese or spinach and cheese)

¼ cup (60 ml) extra-virgin olive oil, plus more as needed

1 head escarole, cored and washed, roughly cut into 1-inch (2.5-cm) bite-sized pieces

Freshly ground pepper, to taste

1 clove garlic, finely grated

Grated Parmigiano-Reggiano or local cheese with a hard and sharp profile, to garnish

Freshly squeeze one or two blood oranges (depending on the size), to yield ¼ cup (60 ml) of juice, and set aside. Discard the squeezed oranges.

Halve the remaining blood orange crosswise. Take one half and slice it into thin rounds about ¼ inch (6 mm) thick and set aside. Cut the remaining half into thin wedges to pass at the table; set aside.

Bring a large pot of water to a boil. Generously salt and add the ravioli. Cook the ravioli according to the package directions, usually just until they all begin to float to the surface of the water. Reserve 1 tablespoon (15 ml) of the cooking water before draining. Drain well.

In the meantime, add the olive oil to a large 12-inch (30-cm) skillet over low heat. When hot and shimmery, add the orange slices, allowing them to sit undisturbed to slightly caramelize, then turn and do the same on the other side, about 6 minutes total. Use tongs or a slotted spoon to transfer the slices to a plate and set aside.

Add the escarole to the olive oil in the skillet, lightly season with salt and pepper and cook until slightly wilted, about 1 minute. Add the garlic and gently stir until fragrant, 30 seconds. Add the freshly squeezed juice and scrape the bottom of the pan to deglaze any flavorful brown bits that may have accumulated; the liquid will emulsify a bit as you stir. Continue to cook the liquid for roughly 1 minute more and turn off the heat. It's fine if the ravioli needs another minute to cook; the mixture can sit until ready.

Add the ravioli to the skillet along with the reserved pasta water. Gently toss to coat. If it's necessary to loosen the ravioli more, drizzle with more olive oil.

To serve, add the ravioli and the escarole to individual plates. Top with freshly ground pepper, grated cheese and the caramelized orange slices. The flesh of the caramelized oranges can be cut into and enjoyed with the ravioli and the peel can be discarded. However, if the oranges were caramelized well, you might also find the caramelized peel enjoyable.

Serve with orange wedges at the table for anyone who would like a fresh squeeze of juice, and a more pronounced flavor, on their ravioli.

Pasta e Patate (Pasta with Potato)

Pasta with potato is a dish that is native to both Southern Italy and to my childhood. This was a common after-school dish when the weather turned cold. The aroma of onions and potatoes simmering in fragrant broth is nostalgic, and if I close my eyes, I can see my grandmother stirring her pot with the same wooden spoon that I use now. I prefer a small pasta like lumachine so that I can enjoy this in heaping spoonfuls. Pasta with potatoes has all the cozy elements that a piping hot bowl of pasta should have on a blustery day.

Serves 4–6

3 tbsp (45 ml) extra-virgin olive oil, plus more for drizzling

1 small onion, roughly chopped

1 tbsp (18 g) kosher salt, plus more for cooking onion

5 cups (1.2 L) low-sodium chicken broth, plus more as needed

1 small clove garlic, finely grated

2 medium yellow or white potatoes, peeled and diced

3 tbsp (45 ml) tomato sauce

12 oz (340 g) lumachine or conchiglie (or other small pasta like ditalini)

¼-lb (113-g) chunk provolone cheese, cubed

Freshly ground black pepper, to taste

In a large, roughly 4-quart (4-L) pot over low–medium heat, add the olive oil. When the oil is hot and shimmery, add the onion, lightly season with salt and cook until tender and beginning to caramelize, 8 to 10 minutes.

In another medium saucepan, add the broth and bring to a simmer.

Add the garlic to the onions and stir, cooking until fragrant, about 30 seconds.

Add the potatoes, the tomato sauce and the hot broth, and season with the salt. Stir well. Deglaze the pan by scraping up any flavorful brown bits that may have accumulated. Bring the contents to a low boil, cover and cook for 8 to 10 minutes.

Uncover and add the pasta. Keep the broth at a low boil and cook, stirring often, until the pasta is a minute or two shy of al dente, tender yet firm to the bite, about 10 minutes. The liquid should be mostly, though not entirely, absorbed, and the potatoes should be tender. If not, continue to cook for another minute or two. The pasta should be very fluid. Add more warm broth, if needed, to loosen. Taste and adjust the seasonings if necessary.

Remove the pot from the heat and add the cubes of provolone, briefly and gently toss, and then let the pot sit for a moment to allow the warmth of the pasta to soften and melt the cheese just so. The pasta will continue to thicken significantly as it stands and is best enjoyed right away.

Serve in individual bowls, topping with freshly ground pepper and a light drizzle of olive oil.

Cook's Notes: *This is a great recipe to use up any leftover tomato sauce or handfuls of small mixed pastas, "pasta mista," from the pantry. If you'd prefer a less melted cheese, swap the provolone for shavings of Parmigiano-Reggiano.*

Creamy Lemon Pappardelle

This is an easy and elegant weeknight dinner that makes the most of winter's lemons. Just a few simple ingredients, likely ones you'll already have on hand, is all that is needed to create a light and bright simple dinner. While there is no heavy cream in this dish, there is a good splash of half and half. The secret to making this dish creamy is the addition of fresh lemon juice at the end. The technique of quickly tossing the pasta off the heat, while adding lemon juice in a slow stream, will thicken the dairy, creating a luxuriously creamy dish. Enjoy this dish alone or paired with roasted chicken.

Serves 2–4

2 small organic lemons, zested and freshly squeezed (2 tbsp [30 ml] of juice)

Kosher salt, to taste

12 oz (340 g) pappardelle

2 tbsp (30 ml) extra-virgin olive oil, plus more for drizzling

1 small onion, thinly sliced

1 cup (240 ml) half and half

Freshly ground pepper, to taste

Grated Parmigiano-Reggiano or local cheese with a hard and sharp profile, to garnish

Finely zest the lemons, setting the zest aside. Juice the lemons and set the juice aside. Discard the lemons.

Bring a large pot of water to a boil. Generously salt and then add the pasta. Cook until just shy of al dente, tender yet firm to the bite, according to the package directions. Reserve 1 cup (240 ml) of the pasta water before draining. Drain well.

In the meantime, add the olive oil to a large 12-inch (30-cm) skillet over low-medium heat. When the oil is hot and shimmery, add the onion. Lightly season with salt and sauté, stirring often, until the onion is tender and begins to caramelize, about 10 minutes.

Lower the heat to a simmer and add the lemon zest and the half and half to the skillet. Season with salt and pepper and stir to combine. Cook to thoroughly heat through, about 1 minute.

Add ¼ cup (60 ml) of the reserved pasta water to the skillet and stir to mix well. Add the pasta and toss to coat. Continue to toss and simmer until some of the liquid has absorbed and the pasta has finished cooking, 1 to 2 minutes. Remove the skillet from the heat and, while working quickly and constantly, toss the pasta while adding 2 tablespoons (30 ml) of the lemon juice in a slow stream. Continue to toss after the juice has been added to ensure an even mix. The pasta should be creamy and silky, not sticky or pasty. If the sauce feels too creamy and you'd like it thinned out more, add a splash more of the reserved pasta water to loosen, tossing the pasta again to coat well. The pasta will continue to thicken upon standing. It is helpful to keep any remaining pasta water on hand to thin the sauce out further, if necessary.

Top each serving with freshly ground pepper and grated cheese.

Cook's Notes: *When an acid, like lemon juice, is added to dairy, a natural chemical reaction occurs that could curdle the milk. It's important to toss the pasta continuously, while adding the lemon juice in slowly, to control the temperature reaction and prevent curdling.*

Linguine with Butter-Roasted Tomato Sauce

When winter ingredients are scarce, I reach for canned organic San Marzano tomatoes. When slow roasted in butter and garlic, the tomatoes caramelize and thicken up, becoming almost jammy. The garlic softens and sweetens and the heat from the red pepper flakes creates a desirable kick for a sauce that is very Arrabiata-esque. This recipe is easily adaptable if you prefer less heat though—simply lessen or omit the red pepper flakes and decrease the garlic to the desired amount. Play around with the recipe too by adding frozen peas or briny capers, or both. The sauce creates an aroma that will waft through the entire house and, for me, that is reason enough to make this dish on a winter's night.

Serves 4–6

1 (28-oz [794-g]) can whole peeled San Marzano tomatoes (with juices)

4 small cloves garlic, smashed

4 tbsp (60 g) butter, cut into small pieces

½ tsp crushed red pepper flakes, plus more for serving

Kosher salt and freshly ground pepper, to taste

1 lb (454 g) linguine (or other long pasta of choice)

½ cup (120 ml) half and half

Grated Parmigiano-Reggiano or local cheese with a hard and sharp profile, to garnish

Preheat the oven to 425°F (220°C).

Trim the stemmed ends off the tomatoes, if any, and discard. Lightly crush the tomatoes by hand, or use a square-head potato masher, and add the tomatoes to a large 9 x 13-inch (23 x 33-cm) baking dish along with the juices.

Add the garlic, butter and red pepper flakes. Season well with salt and a few turns of fresh pepper, then mix to combine. Place the baking dish in the oven and roast until the mixture thickens and the garlic softens, 35 to 40 minutes.

Remove from the oven and, using a fork or a square-head potato masher, break up the garlic. Scrape up any flavorful brown bits that may have accumulated on the bottom and sides of the baking dish, and stir them to incorporate.

Meanwhile, bring a large pot of water to a boil. Generously salt the water and add the pasta. Cook until just shy of al dente, tender yet firm to the bite, according to the package directions. Reserve ½ cup (120 ml) of the pasta water before draining. Drain well.

Return the pasta to the pot and add the roasted tomato sauce and the reserved pasta water, tossing well, 2 to 3 minutes. Turn the heat to a simmer to keep the pasta hot and add the half and half. Gently toss again until the pasta absorbs some of the liquid and finishes cooking, about 1 minute. Remove the pot from the heat.

Divide the pasta into individual portions and top with grated cheese and more red pepper flakes, if desired.

Pasta with Lentils

Lentils (lenticchie) are a great ingredient to add meaty substance to an otherwise simple pasta dish. Lentils are also known for absorbing all the wonderful flavors of the meal they inhabit: in this case, dry red wine, canned tomatoes and vegetable broth. As children, my grandmother would make this for us on cold afternoons, served with warm crusty bread and butter. You can customize this further with the addition of fresh kale or escarole. Traditionally, broken noodles are used, or a mix of leftover tiny pastas from the pantry. The choice is yours. No matter your age though, pasta with lentils is a warm bowl of comfort that will fill and satisfy your belly and soul.

Serves 4–6

1½ tbsp (27 g) kosher salt, plus more for cooking pasta

1 lb (454 g) linguine, broken into approximately 3-inch (7.5-cm) pieces

3 cups (720 ml) vegetable broth

½ cup (100 g) lentils

3 tbsp (45 ml) extra-virgin olive oil, plus more for drizzling

1 large clove garlic, finely grated

1 (28-oz [794-g]) can whole San Marzano tomatoes, lightly crushed, with juices

½ cup (120 ml) dry red wine

Coarsely ground fresh pepper, to taste

Red pepper flakes, to garnish

Grated Parmigiano-Reggiano or local cheese with a hard and sharp profile, to garnish

Bring a large pot of water to a boil. Generously salt the water and add the pasta. Cook until just shy of al dente, tender but firm to the bite, according to the package directions. Reserve 1 cup (240 ml) of the pasta water before draining. Drain well.

Meanwhile, in a large 12-inch (30-cm) skillet with deep sides, add the broth and bring to a boil over high heat. Add the lentils and stir to mix. Lower the heat to medium and cover, cooking until the lentils are almost tender, about 20 minutes.

To the skillet add the olive oil, garlic, tomatoes with their juices and red wine. Season with 1½ tablespoons (27 g) of salt and roughly ten turns of freshly ground pepper. Reduce the heat to low and simmer, stirring often, until the contents have warmed through and the lentils are fully tender, 5 to 10 minutes more. The mixture will look very watery at this point—the pasta will absorb almost all of it and it will continue to thicken up as it sits.

Add the pasta to the skillet, along with ¼ cup (60 ml) of the reserved pasta water, reserving the rest. Gently mix until much of the liquid is absorbed, about 2 minutes. Cover and let the pasta rest for another 5 to 10 minutes to absorb more of the residual liquid, noting that there should be enough liquid left to keep fluidity and to easily be enjoyed with a fork; this shouldn't be soupy. Taste and adjust the seasonings if necessary. Use the reserved pasta water only to loosen the pasta, if needed.

To serve, divide among individual serving bowls. Drizzle with extra-virgin olive oil, top with red pepper flakes (if a little heat is desired) and a generous grating of cheese.

Pappardelle with Chorizo Bolognese

In the diverse cultural community in northern New Jersey, where I grew up, many quality ethnic family markets dotted our main avenue, and it was there where we discovered the spicy, peppery goodness of chorizo, both fresh and dried. In this recipe, I'm using fresh chorizo with its distinctive tang and gorgeous deep red color. I've paired it with ground beef to balance the tanginess and added fire-roasted tomatoes, roasting them myself during tomato season and utilizing the canned variety in the colder months. Pappardelle is the perfect thick-ribbon pasta to sweep it all up. Red wine and capers add fragrance to the sauce, and fresh burrata provides the perfect finishing touch.

Serves 4–6

Kosher salt, to taste

1 lb (454 g) pappardelle

3 tbsp (45 ml) extra-virgin olive oil

1 small onion, finely diced

½ lb (225 g) fresh-ground beef

½ lb (225 g) fresh-ground chorizo; if whole, remove and discard casings

1 clove garlic, finely grated

Freshly ground pepper, to taste

1 cup (240 ml) dry red wine

1 (28-oz [794-g]) can fire-roasted tomatoes, diced

2 tbsp (20 g) capers, rinsed and drained

Fresh burrata cheese, room temperature

Bring a large pot of water to a boil. Generously salt the water and add the pasta. Cook until just shy of al dente, tender yet firm to the bite, according to the package directions. Reserve ½ cup (120 ml) of the pasta water before draining. Drain well.

Meanwhile, in a large 13- to 15-inch (33- to 38-cm) skillet, heat the olive oil over low-medium heat. When the oil is hot and shimmery, add the onion, beef, chorizo, garlic, salt and pepper. Cook, stirring frequently and breaking up the pieces of meat with a fork or your cooking spoon until fully cooked through and the onion is tender: 10 to 15 minutes, depending on the size of the ground pieces.

Remove the skillet from the heat to add the wine, then return to moderate heat and bring to a boil, cooking until the wine is reduced by half, 3 to 5 minutes. Add the tomatoes and bring to a boil. Cook, stirring often, until most of the liquid has reduced by half, about 5 minutes. Add the capers and briefly stir to incorporate.

Add the pasta and ¼ cup (60 ml) of the reserved pasta water to the skillet, tossing well to coat and absorb some of the liquid, 1 minute. Use the remaining reserved pasta water to loosen the pasta only if necessary—otherwise discard.

To serve, divide among individual serving plates and top with fresh burrata and a few turns of ground pepper.

Pasta with Fried Eggs

This dish really couldn't be simpler to prepare, but it is big on taste. I lean on this dish when I don't know what to make or when I'm low on other ingredients and I need to feed my family in a hurry. A few kitchen staples and a large skillet is all you will need. Garlic and red pepper flakes add just the right amount of heat and the toasted flakes dot the eggs' whites for high-impact flavor. No worries though—just reduce or omit the red pepper flakes if you prefer less heat. The longest part of the preparation is waiting for the water to boil.

Serves 4

Kosher salt

12 oz (340 g) fettucine

¼ cup (60 ml) extra-virgin olive oil, plus more to drizzle

1 tbsp (15 g) butter

3 large cloves garlic, smashed and peeled

4-6 eggs

¼ tsp red pepper flakes

Freshly ground pepper, to taste

Grated pecorino cheese or local cheese with a hard and sharp profile, to garnish

Bring a large pot of water to a boil. Generously salt the water and add the pasta. Cook until just shy of al dente, tender yet firm to the bite, according to the package directions. Reserve ½ cup (120 ml) of the pasta water before draining. Drain well.

In the meantime, in a skillet over low-medium heat, add the olive oil, butter and garlic. Cook the garlic to release its flavor, stirring often. When it is lightly golden on both sides, about 3 minutes, use a slotted spoon to remove the garlic pieces and discard.

Reduce the heat to low. Taking caution with the hot oil, crack each egg one at a time, carefully adding them to the oil; do not scramble, just slip them in and allow them to fry. Season with red pepper flakes. When the whites are just about set and the yolks are still a tad runny, add the pasta and ¼ cup (60 ml) of the reserved pasta water to the skillet. Toss together, gently breaking up the whites as you toss. The heat from the pasta will assist in completely cooking the eggs. Only use the remaining pasta water to loosen the pasta if necessary.

To serve, add a few turns of freshly ground pepper and a drizzle of oil. Serve with a generous grating of cheese.

Leftover Frittata di Pasta

Turn a leftover serving or two of pasta into an entirely new meal with the addition of just a few common pantry staples. Depending on how much you are using though, you may have to adjust the quantity of eggs. There's no rule here other than making sure to have enough eggs to adequately coat the pasta, while still allowing some of the pasta to peek through a bit so the tips can crisp up. Unlike many frittata recipes that are thick and quiche-like, this recipe is meant to be thin and crisp on the outside. Adapt this recipe with the changing seasons by serving the frittata over a bed of seasonal greens that have been simply dressed in extra-virgin olive oil and lemon. This dish tastes best at room temperature.

Serves 4

4 eggs

3 tbsp (15 g) grated Parmigiano-Reggiano or local cheese with a hard and sharp profile, plus more for sprinkling

Kosher salt and freshly ground pepper, to taste

Leftover pasta with sauce (at least ⅔ lb [300 g]) (see Cook's Notes)

2 tbsp (30 g) tomato paste

2 tbsp (30 ml) extra-virgin olive oil, plus more for drizzling

Red pepper flakes, to taste (optional)

Beat the eggs in a bowl that is large enough to also accommodate the pasta.

Add the grated cheese, a sprinkle of salt and a few turns of freshly ground pepper, and beat again. Add the leftover pasta to the eggs, along with the tomato paste, and mix well to coat every strand.

To a large 12-inch (30-cm) oven-safe skillet, add the olive oil over low–medium heat. When the oil is hot and shimmery, add a sprinkle of red pepper flakes, if using, and let them sit to toast, 1 minute. Add the pasta and egg mixture, giving the contents a gentle stir to lightly incorporate the oil. Spread the pasta out evenly. You'll notice some of the oil pooling around the edges; that's fine, as it will absorb into the pasta as it cooks and cools. Cook until the bottom of the pasta begins to toast and crisp and the eggs have begun to set, about 5 minutes.

After toasting the bottom, sprinkle the frittata with a good handful of Parmigiano and place the pan under a broiler set to high. Broil until the top begins to crisp and the eggs have cooked through, roughly 3 to 4 minutes. Keep a watchful eye as broiler temperatures vary; take care not to burn.

Allow the frittata to cool before serving. To serve, lightly drizzle the top with more olive oil and simply cut into slices like a pie. This dish tastes best slightly warm or at room temperature.

Cook's Notes: *You can use any kind of leftover pasta like traditional marinara or carbonara. Get creative! Consider adding thinly sliced meats or greens to the pasta and egg mixture.*

One-Pot Cheesy Spaghetti Bake

I don't know what I love most about this dish, the warm layer of toasted and melted mozzarella, the way the tips of the pasta crisp up ever-so-slightly when broiled or that it all comes together in just one pot. This recipe pairs beautifully with a warm slice of rustic bread and your favorite wine. Whether or not you want to enjoy it curled up on the sofa or in front of the fire is entirely up to you.

Serves 4–6

3 tbsp (45 ml) extra-virgin olive oil, plus more for drizzling

¼ tsp red pepper flakes

1 small onion, roughly diced

Kosher salt

2 cloves garlic, finely grated

1 cup (240 ml) white wine

4 cups (1 L) chicken broth, plus 1 cup (240 ml) extra, if needed

2 tsp (10 g) dry Italian seasonings (mix of garlic powder, basil, oregano, rosemary, savory, etc.)

Freshly ground pepper, to taste

1 lb (454 g) spaghetti, broken in half

1 tbsp (15 g) butter

2 cups (224 g) grated mozzarella cheese or more as desired

Grated Parmigiano-Reggiano or local cheese with a hard and sharp profile, to garnish

In a large enameled cast-iron pot, at least 5 quarts (5 L), heat the olive oil over low–medium heat until hot and shimmery. Add the red pepper flakes and cook until they are toasted, 1 minute.

Add the onion and sprinkle with salt. Sauté, stirring often, until the onion is tender and lightly caramelized, about 10 minutes. Add the garlic and stir until fragrant, 30 seconds.

Remove the pot from the heat to add the wine, then return to moderate heat and scrape the bottom to deglaze any flavorful brown bits that may have accumulated. Stir to incorporate all the ingredients.

Add the broth, Italian seasonings and salt and pepper to taste, then stir to mix. Bring to a boil and add the uncooked spaghetti. Stir often to prevent sticking. Keep extra broth on hand and add it if the spaghetti absorbs too much liquid.

Cook the pasta until 1 minute shy of al dente, tender yet firm to the bite, about 10 to 13 minutes. The pasta should be creamy with movement, not soupy. Add the butter and stir to mix.

Top the spaghetti evenly with the mozzarella and place the pot under a broiler set to high heat. Broil until the cheese is melted, bubbling and beginning to brown in some spots, 2 minutes or so—broilers vary, so keep a watchful eye.

To serve, scoop into individual bowls, drizzle with olive oil and garnish with grated cheese.

Rigatoni with Dark Cocoa and Red Wine Short Rib Ragu

Don't make the mistake of thinking this is a chocolate-y or sweet pasta dish—it's not. Not even close. Savory and enchanting? Absolutely. The cocoa bean is quite bitter on its own and is rightfully considered a spice—though it is far underrepresented in the kitchen other than when it is sweetened for baking. When combined, red wine, beef stock and dark cocoa add a deep and rich complexity to braised meat and a succulent, almost indescribable, flavor. This dish has long been a family favorite and is one of the most accessed recipes on my blog. The added benefit of a braised dish like this is the aroma—the entire house will be blanketed with the percolating scent of wine, warm chocolate and spice.

Serves 4–6

1 (28-oz [794-g]) can San Marzano tomatoes, whole and peeled (with juices)

3 lbs (1.4 kg) boneless short ribs

Kosher salt and freshly ground pepper, to taste

⅓ cup (49 g) all-purpose unbleached organic flour

2 tbsp (30 ml) extra-virgin olive oil

5 oz (142 g) chopped pancetta

1 medium onion, diced

3 cloves garlic, finely grated

2 tbsp (30 g) tomato paste

2½ cups (590 ml) beef stock

1 cup (240 ml) dry red wine

1 tsp chopped fresh rosemary leaves

1 tsp dried thyme

½ tsp dried oregano

1 bay leaf

3 tbsp (15 g) natural and/or Dutch-blend cocoa powder, unsweetened

1 lb (454 g) rigatoni

4-6 tsp (10-15 g) 100% cacao unsweetened chocolate, bar, grated, to garnish

Parmigiano–Reggiano or grated local cheese with a hard and sharp profile, to garnish

Add the tomatoes to a large bowl with their juices. Use clean hands or a square-head potato masher to lightly crush the tomatoes. Set aside.

Trim the fat from both sides of the ribs, being mindful to leave the thick fibrous tissue intact that holds it together. Generously season the ribs with salt and pepper and dredge in flour, shaking off any excess, and set aside.

Add the oil to a 7-quart (7-L) (or larger) pot or Dutch oven over medium heat. Add the pancetta and toss until crisp, 5 to 6 minutes. Use a slotted spoon to transfer the pancetta to a bowl and set aside.

Add the onion and the short ribs to the pot and cook until the ribs are brown on both sides and the onion is tender, 8 minutes total.

Add the tomatoes, garlic and tomato paste to the pot with the short ribs and give everything a stir, lifting and moving around and under the short ribs. Add the pancetta back to the pot along with the stock, red wine, rosemary, thyme, oregano, bay leaf and cocoa powder. Stir again to combine, and scrape up under the ribs to deglaze any flavorful brown bits that may have accumulated. Bring the contents to a full boil; then reduce to a simmer, cover with a fitted lid and cook for 1 hour and 30 minutes.

Remove the lid and simmer for 1 hour and 15 minutes longer, stirring occasionally. During the last 20 minutes of simmering, bring a separate large pot of water to a boil. Generously salt the water and add the pasta. Cook until just shy of al dente, tender yet firm to the bite, according to the package directions. Reserve 2 cups (480 ml) of the pasta water before draining. Drain well.

Carefully shred the meat in the pot (using two forks to pull the meat apart). Taste and adjust the seasonings, if necessary.

Add the pasta along with ¼ cup (60 ml) of the reserved pasta water to the pot with the short ribs, tossing gently to combine. If more moisture is needed, add more of the reserved pasta water, ¼ cup (60 ml) at a time. The meal should be thick and hearty, while retaining movement, and not sticky or pasty.

Transfer the pasta and short ribs to individual serving bowls. Garnish each bowl with approximately 1 teaspoon of the grated unsweetened chocolate and a generous amount of grated cheese. Serve hot.

Cioppino Pasta

Cioppino is a San Francisco–style seafood stew. We make this meal every Christmas Eve as part of the traditional Italian Feast of the Seven Fishes, using four of the fishes in this dish alone. I prefer to serve this with a medium-sized pasta like casarecce with its scroll-like bends and folds, cupping all that wonderful flavor. Make sure to serve this dish with a good crusty bread to mop up all the fragrant broth.

Serves 4–6

Kosher salt

1 lb (454 g) casarecce (substitute with strozzapreti or any other twisted tube-like pasta)

¼ cup (60 ml) extra-virgin olive oil

½ tsp crushed red pepper flakes

1 medium onion, thinly sliced

1 (6-oz [170-g]) can tomato paste

4 cloves garlic, finely grated

1 cup (240 ml) Sauvignon Blanc

1 (28-oz [794-g]) can whole peeled San Marzano tomatoes (with juices), lightly crushed

3 cups (720 ml) fish stock

2 bay leaves

24 small littleneck clams, shells cleaned

24 mussels (about 1½ lbs [680 g]), debearded

20 large shrimp, cleaned

1 lb (454 g) halibut, cut into 2-inch (5-cm) chunks

Bring a large pot of water to a boil. Generously salt the water and add the pasta. Cook until about 1 minute shy of al dente, tender yet firm to the bite, according to the package directions. Reserve ½ cup (120 ml) of the pasta water before draining. Drain well.

Meanwhile, in a large 15-inch (38-cm) skillet, with deep sides and a tight-fitting lid (or have foil on hand to tightly cover), heat the olive oil over low–medium heat. Add the red pepper flakes and the onion, and lightly season with salt. Cook, stirring often, until the onion is tender and beginning to caramelize, 10 minutes. Push the onion to the sides of the pan and add the tomato paste to the center, the hot spot, of the skillet and let it sit for roughly 2 minutes to caramelize. Stir the paste in to incorporate it into the onion. Add the garlic, stirring until fragrant, 30 seconds.

Remove the skillet from the heat to add the wine, then return to low–medium heat, scraping to deglaze any flavorful brown pieces that may have accumulated. Add the tomatoes with their juices, fish stock and bay leaves, and stir well. Simmer to let the flavors come together, about 2 minutes.

Add the clams and mussels to the skillet. Cover and cook until the clams and mussels just begin to open, about 5 minutes. Add the shrimp and halibut. Continue to simmer until the shrimp and fish have cooked through and the shellfish have fully opened, about 5 minutes more. If any of the shellfish have not opened, give them a gentle stir and cover for another minute. If any of the shellfish still have not opened, discard them.

Add the pasta and ¼ cup (60 ml) of the reserved pasta water. Gently and briefly toss to combine, taking care not to break apart the fish, and to finish cooking the pasta, about 1 minute. Only use the rest of the reserved water if needed to thin the sauce, which should be like a thick broth, loose but not watery.

To serve, divide into individual bowls. Pass more red pepper flakes at the table. Serve with a rustic crusty bread.

Cook's Notes: *Discard any shellfish that are opened when you receive them and do not close on their own while rinsing and cleaning (this means they are no longer alive).*

Aletria (Portuguese Holiday Dessert)

Aletria, with its light, creamy and almost pudding-like texture, subtly hinted with lemon and warm cinnamon spice, is a classic Portuguese Christmas dessert made with thin pasta. I grew up in a diverse cultural community, and my high school best friend, Christine, lived in a predominantly Portuguese neighborhood one town over. Her grandmother made an out-of-this-world sweet dessert that I knew I'd have to include in this cookbook. I'm fortunate that Christine and another Portuguese friend, Hilda, were both kind enough to share their family's recipes with me. It is worth noting that, like most cultural recipes, Aletria seems to vary a bit between families. This version is soft, creamy and loose, but still able to be scooped while mostly retaining its shape. I hope to have honored this wonderful dish. It has a very special place in my memories and heart.

Serves 6

6 angel hair pasta nests, about 8½ oz (245 g), gently untangled

4½ cups (1.1 L) whole milk, plus more if needed

3 egg yolks

½ cup (120 ml) water

1 cup (200 g) sugar

1 lemon rind, about a 3-inch (7.5-cm) piece

4 tbsp (60 g) butter

Ground cinnamon, to garnish

Gently untangle the angel hair noodles and set aside; it's fine if they break.

Beat ½ cup (120 ml) of milk with the egg yolks to combine. Set aside in a small bowl.

In a large saucepan over moderate heat, add the remaining 4 cups (1 L) of milk and the water. Heat just until the mixture begins to boil, then add the sugar, lemon rind and butter to the saucepan. Stir gently until the sugar dissolves (you'll no longer feel the grittiness of the sugar at the bottom of the pan), about 5 minutes. Remove the lemon rind and discard.

Reduce the heat to medium and add the angel hair noodles, and stir to mix well. Cook the noodles, stirring often, until tender, 6 to 7 minutes. Taste. If the noodles still have a slight crunch, cook for another minute longer. If the noodles appear to have absorbed too much of the cooking liquid, add more milk—just enough for the noodles to be able to continue cooking until tender.

Meanwhile, in a separate medium bowl, temper the egg yolk mixture by very slowly streaming in 3 tablespoons (45 ml) of the hot milk from the pot while simultaneously and vigorously stirring to prevent the eggs from scrambling. Continue stirring until mixed well.

Lower the heat to a simmer and slowly add the tempered eggs to the saucepan, while continuing to quickly stir. Continue to stir until well incorporated and warmed through, less than 1 minute. Turn off the heat. The mixture should appear very loose. Note that it will begin to thicken almost immediately off the heat and will continue to thicken as it cools.

Pour the pasta mixture into a rectangular 2.2-quart (2-L) baking dish. Sprinkle the top with the ground cinnamon—many families add the cinnamon in a lattice design, though some families will use holiday cut outs or doilies to make more intricate cinnamon designs. Plan to make this and let it sit at room temperature for at least several hours before serving. Serve by scooping into individual serving dishes.

Tagliatelle with Vanilla-Champagne Butter Sauce

Don't be fooled by the title. This is a savory dish, not sweet. I usually make this as part of my New Year's Eve festivities, when the champagne is already flowing. It ties the celebratory theme in nicely, though it tastes just as wonderful any time of the year. It couldn't be easier to prepare—the sauce is ready by the time the pasta has finished boiling. The warm floral undertone of vanilla is subtle, adding its dark brown specks to the tagliatelle, balanced perfectly by the caramelized shallots and onions. The champagne reduces to an essence, reminiscent of a white wine, and the splash of cream gives this dish body. Enjoy this as-is or consider adding shrimp or pairing with your favorite chicken recipe for a more substantial meal.

Serves 4–6

Kosher salt

1 lb (454 g) tagliatelle

¼ cup (60 ml) extra-virgin olive oil, plus more for drizzling

1 small onion, sliced thin

1 shallot, sliced thin

½ cup (120 ml) brut champagne

1 vanilla bean

1 cup (240 ml) light cream

2 tbsp (30 g) butter

Freshly ground pepper, to taste

Grated Parmigiano-Reggiano or local cheese with a hard and sharp profile, to garnish

Bring a large pot of water to a boil. Generously salt and add the pasta. Cook until just shy of al dente, tender yet firm to the bite, according to the package directions. Reserve 1 cup (240 ml) of the pasta water before draining. Drain well.

In the meantime, in a large 12-inch (30-cm) skillet over low–medium heat, heat the olive oil until hot and shimmery. Add the onion and shallot and lightly season with salt. Sauté, stirring often, until the onion and shallot are tender and beginning to caramelize, about 10 minutes. Remove the skillet from the heat to add the champagne. Scrape the seeds from both sides of the halved vanilla bean. Add the seeds to the skillet and discard the pods. Return the pan to moderate heat and deglaze the pot by scraping up any flavorful brown bits that may have accumulated. Bring the contents to a low boil and cook, stirring often, until the champagne reduces by half, about 5 minutes.

Reduce the heat to low and add the light cream. Cook until the sauce thickens just slightly, enough to lightly coat the back of a spoon, 3 to 5 minutes.

Add the pasta and ¼ cup (60 ml) of the reserved pasta water to the skillet. Toss until the pasta is well coated and has finished cooking, about 1 minute. Use more reserved pasta water to thin the sauce, if necessary. The texture should be silky and creamy.

Add the butter and gently toss until the butter is melted and the sauce has a glossy finish, 1 minute. Season with salt and a few turns of freshly ground pepper, to taste.

To serve, divide into individual bowls and top with grated cheese and a light drizzle of olive oil. Serve immediately. The pasta will thicken upon standing.

Fresh Fettuccine with Roasted Parsnips in White Wine Cream

When parsnips are roasted, they become soft and sweet and make for a wonderful addition to pasta. Feel free to prepare the parsnips a few hours in advance and toss them in at room temperature—the heat from the pasta and sauce will help to warm them through.

Serves 4–6

2 lb (907 g) parsnips, peeled, quartered lengthwise, cored, then cut crosswise into ¼-inch (6-mm) pieces

3 tbsp (45 ml) extra-virgin olive oil, divided, plus more for drizzling

Kosher salt and freshly ground pepper, to taste

1 lb (454 g) fresh fettuccine (page 16)

4 oz (112 g) diced pancetta

1 medium leek, thinly sliced

½ cup (120 ml) Sauvignon Blanc

½ cup (120 ml) half and half

⅓ cup (35 g) grated Parmigiano-Reggiano or local cheese with a hard and sharp profile, plus more to garnish

Preheat the oven to 400°F (200°C).

Line a baking sheet with parchment paper or a silicone mat. Place the cut parsnips on the baking sheet and drizzle with 2 tablespoons (30 ml) of the olive oil. Season well with salt and freshly ground pepper and massage onto the parsnips. Roast until the parsnips are tender, about 25 minutes, tossing once halfway through.

Meanwhile, bring a large pot of water to a boil. Generously salt and add the pasta. Note that fresh pasta cooks quickly, in 1 to 2 minutes. Reserve 1 cup (240 ml) of the pasta water before draining. Drain well.

In a large 12-inch (30-cm) skillet with deep sides over medium–high heat, add 1 tablespoon (15 ml) of olive oil and pancetta and toss until crisp, 5 to 6 minutes. Use a slotted spoon to transfer the pancetta to a paper towel–lined plate to drain any excess oil, leaving behind as much oil as possible in the skillet.

Lower the heat to moderate, then add the leek. Cook until the leek is soft and beginning to caramelize, about 10 minutes. Add the pancetta back to the skillet. Remove the skillet from the heat to add the wine. Return to low heat and scrape the bottom of the pan to deglaze any flavorful brown bits that may have accumulated. Simmer for 2 minutes. Add the half and half. Simmer until just slightly thickened, about 3 minutes.

Add the pasta to the skillet along with ¼ cup (60 ml) of the reserved pasta water. Turn off the heat. Add the parsnips and slowly sprinkle in the grated cheese while quickly tossing to mix and melt the cheese—and to help prevent it from sticking to the bottom. Season with salt to taste.

Use the remaining pasta water, ¼ cup (60 ml) at a time, only to loosen the mixture if it has thickened up too much. The pasta should be fluid and creamy, not pasty.

To serve, divide into individual bowls and drizzle lightly with olive oil and a few turns of freshly ground pepper. Garnish with more grated cheese.

Fresh Chestnut Pasta with Sausage

In Italy, grinding chestnuts into a flour was historically associated with peasants who could not afford wheat flour. Nowadays it is an elegant seasonal alternative to traditional pasta. I've made an adaptation by adding a rough puree of chestnuts into my pasta dough. The chestnuts impart an earthiness to the pasta and evoke a warm taste of winter.

Serves 4–6

12 chestnuts

½ cup (120 ml) milk, or more as needed

½ cup (120 ml) water

Basic Pasta Dough (page 16)

3 tbsp (45 ml) extra-virgin olive oil, plus more for drizzling

10 sage leaves

1 lb (454 g) sweet Italian sausage, casings removed

1 clove garlic, finely grated

⅓ cup (80 ml) Sauvignon Blanc

1 cup (240 ml) half and half

Kosher salt and freshly ground pepper, to taste

Grated Parmigiano-Reggiano or local cheese with a hard and sharp profile, to garnish

With a sharp knife, make an "x" on the flat side of each chestnut, taking care to fully pierce the skin and not the chestnut.

In a medium saucepan, add the milk, water and chestnuts. Make sure the chestnuts are fully submerged; if they are not, add a bit more milk. Simmer the chestnuts over low–medium heat until soft, 30 minutes. Scoop the chestnuts out of the liquid, strain the liquids and set aside. Peel the chestnuts and discard the shells.

Add the peeled chestnuts and ½ cup (120 ml) of the strained liquids to a high-powered blender and puree, making sure the pureed pieces are small, as they will need to fit through the rollers on a pasta machine. Add 1 cup (120 ml) of the puree to the eggs in the Basic Pasta Dough recipe (page 16) and proceed with the directions for preparing fresh pasta.

Bring a large pot of water to a boil.

Meanwhile, to a large 12-inch (30-cm) skillet with deep sides over low–medium heat, add the olive oil. When the oil is hot and shimmery, add the sage leaves. Be careful, as sage leaves tend to pop and sizzle when frying. Fry until the leaves are crisp, 1 to 2 minutes. Use a slotted spoon or tongs to transfer the sage to a paper towel-lined plate to cool.

Raise the heat to medium and add the sausage to the skillet, breaking up any large pieces into bite-sized pieces with a fork or the back of your cooking spoon. Cook, stirring often, until the sausage is browned and cooked through, about 10 minutes. Add the garlic and sauté until fragrant, 30 seconds. Remove the skillet from the heat to add the wine. Return the pan to the heat and scrape the bottom of the pan to deglaze any flavorful brown bits that may have accumulated. Add the half and half. Season with salt and a few good turns of ground pepper. Turn off the heat.

Generously salt the boiling water and add the pasta, noting that fresh pasta cooks much faster than dry, usually within 1 to 2 minutes. Reserve ½ cup (120 ml) of the pasta water before draining. Drain well.

Add the pasta and ¼ cup (60 ml) of the reserved pasta water to the pan, tossing well to coat the pasta, 1 to 2 minutes. Add more pasta water if necessary to loosen the pasta. The consistency should be silky.

To serve, garnish with a drizzle of olive oil, sage leaves (crumbled or whole) and grated cheese.

Fresh Spaghetti with Crisp Salami and Burrata

In this recipe, salami is sliced into thin strips that have been slightly crisped and entwined with strands of fresh spaghetti. It's important to find salami that is free of antibiotics and nitrates, for the best quality and flavor. This is a very simple weeknight dish that is subtly enhanced with white wine and creamy burrata.

Serves 4–6

Basic Pasta Dough (page 16)

Kosher salt, as needed

¼ cup (60 ml) extra-virgin olive oil, plus more for drizzling

1 onion, thinly sliced

8–10 slices Genoa salami (about 3 oz [90 g]), cut into thin strips

¼ cup (60 ml) Sauvignon Blanc

Freshly ground pepper, to taste

4 oz (112 g) burrata cheese (or as much as desired), room temperature

To make fresh spaghetti, see the Basic Pasta Dough recipe and directions (page 16).

Bring a large pot of water to a boil. Generously salt and add the pasta. Note that fresh pasta cooks more quickly than dry, within 1 to 2 minutes. Reserve 1 cup (240 ml) of the pasta water before draining. Drain well.

Meanwhile, in a large 12-inch (30-cm) skillet with deep sides, heat the olive oil over low-medium heat. When the oil is hot and shimmery, add the onion and lightly season with salt (the salami will add more saltiness, so don't overdo it—but don't skip it either, as lightly salting the onions helps them to cook down). Cook, stirring often, until the onion begins to caramelize, 10 minutes.

Add the salami strips to the pan and cook for just 1 minute. The salami should remain soft and pliable yet begin to crisp in some parts. Don't worry if the slices stick together or if some pieces crisp-up a little more than others; it won't affect the result.

Remove the skillet from the heat to add the wine. Scrape the bottom of the pan to deglaze any flavorful brown bits that may have accumulated. Return the pan to moderate heat and cook the wine for 1 to 2 minutes.

Add the pasta and ½ cup (120 ml) of the reserved cooking water to the skillet. Toss well to coat, taking care to lift and fold in the salami, adding more reserved pasta water if needed to loosen the pasta. Add a few good turns of freshly ground pepper. Taste and adjust the seasonings, if necessary.

To serve, dollop the burrata cheese on top. Add an extra drizzle of extra-virgin olive oil, if desired. The pasta will continue to thicken upon standing.

Cook's Notes: *Burrata should be room temperature when serving to optimize its creamy texture, so take it out of the refrigerator about 30 minutes before you plan to serve this dish.*

SPRING

Here in New Jersey, the early days of spring struggle hard against the last breaths of winter. Often, we are caught in the middle, between dark frost-bitten mornings and mild, pleasant afternoons. In time, spring gains momentum and the first harvest is at hand. For many of us, the first harvest is the elusive, pink-tinged ramp. If you happen to see them, act quickly as their season is fleeting. In the time it takes to boil water, you can make a wonderful pasta meal out of them using my recipe for Tagliatelle with Wild Ramps and Aleppo Pepper (page 103).

Soon, asparagus moves up slowly through the dark, damp soil, its arrival trumpeting the beginning of the first main harvest! The farm markets in town that sat quiet and dark all winter long unfurl their "Our Own Fresh Asparagus!" banners that billow in the cool April wind. For me, that officially marks the culinary transition from winter to spring. Just like that, my braising pots are replaced by baking sheets crowded with farm-fresh asparagus spears lightly salted and massaged in olive oil and briefly roasted to perfection. I toss together my Tortellini Salad with Roasted Asparagus Pesto (page 107), hands down one of the easiest and most satisfying ways to welcome early spring.

As the season progresses with milder evenings, our pasta recipes reflect the same, becoming lighter and brighter. One of my most beloved dishes for its ease and simplicity is Spinach and Avocado Linguine (page 128). A quick blend of raw avocado and baby spinach, scented with garlic and a squeeze of bright lemon, is all it takes for this no-cook sauce to coat silky tendrils of linguine, made in less time than it takes to boil pasta water. This is my go-to dish for that first balmy spring evening when dinner simply must go from the stove straight to the patio.

The pasta recipes you'll find in this chapter reflect the mixed temperament of the season and the long-awaited green hues of new life thriving just outside of our doors.

Tagliatelle with Wild Ramps and Aleppo Pepper

Ramps, those elusive and wild onions tinged with soft hues of pink, are often the first of the spring greens to emerge. There's a frenzy that ensues when ramps arrive at the farmers' markets because they are scarce where I live, growing only in the wild under the shade of woods, in areas that no forager would ever reveal, which means they are in high demand. Adding to their attraction is their fleeting season—almost as soon as they arrive, they are gone. I love pairing ramps with pasta, especially a long pasta like tagliatelle that's been dusted in grated cheese, and twisting up heaping forkfuls of this first green of the season.

Serves 4

1 bunch ramps (½ to 1 lb [225–454 g])

Kosher salt, to taste

13½ oz (383 g) tagliatelle

¼ cup (60 ml) extra-virgin olive oil, plus more for drizzling

1 tbsp (15 g) butter

¼ tsp Aleppo pepper, plus more to garnish (substitute with red pepper flakes)

1 tsp fine breadcrumbs, to garnish

Grated local cheese with a hard and sharp profile, or pecorino cheese, to garnish

Clean the ramps by trimming off the roots and discarding the outer silvery skin that covers the bulbs—you'll know it because it will feel slippery to the touch. Roughly slice the white and pink parts, and set them aside. Roughly cut the green leaves once in half, crosswise, and set them aside separately from the white and pink parts.

Bring a large pot of water to a boil. Generously salt the water and add the pasta. Cook until just shy of al dente, tender yet firm to the bite, according to the package directions. Reserve ½ cup (120 ml) of the pasta water before draining. Drain well.

In the meantime, in a large 12-inch (30-cm) skillet with deep sides over moderate heat, heat the olive oil, butter and Aleppo pepper. Allow the pepper to toast in the oil and butter, about 1 minute.

Add only the white and pink parts of the ramps to the skillet, stirring often, until tender and caramelized, taking care not to burn, about 10 minutes. Add the green leaves to the skillet, stirring often until tender, 2 to 3 minutes. Season with a sprinkle of salt and gently stir to combine. Turn off the heat.

Add the pasta and ¼ cup (60 ml) of the reserved pasta water to the skillet and toss well to combine, 1 minute. Add a drizzle of olive oil if needed to loosen the pasta. The pasta should be silky, not pasty or sticky. If the pasta absorbs too much, add the rest of the reserved pasta water. Taste and adjust the seasonings, if necessary.

Garnish each serving with an extra drizzle of olive oil, a pinch of Aleppo pepper (optional), about ¼ tsp of breadcrumbs and grated cheese.

Cook's Notes: *Aleppo pepper is not quite as hot as red pepper flakes, though it is doubly as flavorful! If you cannot find ramps where you live, substitute with leeks, using only the white and light green parts. Be sure to clean them as well.*

Creamy Fettuccine with Asparagus and Morels

Petrichor, that earthy scent when rain first falls on dry earth, is what comes to mind when I'm cooking with spring morels, especially when sautéed in hot butter and shallots. With a splash of heavy cream, freshly grated Parmigiano–Reggiano and long silky strands of fettuccine, this becomes the perfect dish to enjoy when these wild mushrooms are in season.

Serves 4–6

½ lb (225 g) asparagus (6–8 large spears), trimmed

1 tbsp (15 ml) plus ¼ cup (60 ml) extra-virgin olive oil, divided, plus more for drizzling

Kosher salt and freshly ground black pepper, to taste

1 lb (454 g) fettuccine

¼ lb (113 g) fresh morels or ½ oz (14 g) dried morels, rehydrated (liquid reserved; see Cook's Notes)

3 tbsp (45 g) butter

2 shallots, finely chopped

¾ cup (180 ml) vegetable stock

½ cup (120 ml) heavy cream

⅓ cup (15 g) finely grated Parmigiano–Reggiano or local cheese with a hard and sharp profile, to garnish

Cut off and discard the tough ends of the asparagus spears. Cut the spears on the bias into 1-inch (2.5-cm) pieces. Rinse and pat dry.

To roast the asparagus, line a baking pan with parchment paper, spread out the asparagus on the sheet and add 1 tablespoon (15 ml) of olive oil and massage onto the asparagus. Sprinkle with salt and pepper and roast for 10 minutes under the broiler set to high, keeping a watchful eye, as broiler temperatures vary. The asparagus should char a bit here and there, though not burn. Thicker stems may need another minute.

In the meantime, bring a large pot of water to a boil. Generously salt the water and add the pasta. Cook until just shy of al dente, tender yet firm to the bite, according to the package directions. Reserve ½ cup (120 ml) of the pasta water before draining. Drain well.

While the pasta cooks, slice the morels lengthwise.

Add the butter and ¼ cup (60 ml) of olive oil to a large 12-inch (30-cm) skillet with deep sides over moderate heat. When the oil is hot and the butter has melted, add the shallots and morels and cook, stirring often, until the shallots have softened and the morels begin to brown, about 10 minutes. Add the cooked asparagus pieces to the skillet and gently toss. Slowly add the stock and heavy cream, season with salt and pepper, and stir to combine. Let the sauce simmer, 1 minute.

Add the pasta and ¼ cup (60 ml) of the reserved pasta water to the skillet, then gently toss to combine, about 1 minute. Taste and adjust the seasonings if necessary. The sauce will continue to thicken upon standing, so use the remaining pasta water only if needed to loosen the pasta. To serve, drizzle with olive oil and a generous garnish of the grated cheese.

Cook's Notes: *Can't find fresh morels? Don't bypass the dried variety. A little hot water will help to reconstitute them, and their steeping liquid can be added to the water in which you cook the pasta. Plan to let dried morels steep for about 30 minutes.*

Tortellini Salad with Roasted Asparagus Pesto

Asparagus, the king of the spring! When bundled, it even appears crown-like, sitting with such pride. I prefer asparagus when it has been roasted, with its delicate tips crisp and caramelized, and the tough stems tender. In this recipe the stems are cut and divided, becoming the base for a robust pesto. The green leafy spring lettuce, when paired with warm tortellini, wilts ever so slightly while still retaining its pleasant crunch.

Serves 4–6

Kosher salt, to taste

12 oz (340 g) tortellini (preferably with a spinach and ricotta filling)

2 tbsp (30 ml) plus ⅓ cup (80 ml) extra-virgin olive oil, divided, plus more for drizzling

1 lb (454 g) asparagus, ends trimmed

Freshly ground pepper, to taste

1 clove garlic, smashed

¼ cup (30 g) slivered almonds (or substitute with pine nuts or other seeds of choice)

¾ cup (75 g) grated Parmigiano–Reggiano or local cheese with a hard and sharp profile, plus more to garnish

1½ tbsp (22 ml) lemon juice, freshly squeezed, plus more as needed

1 head leafy greens, washed, cored and leaves roughly torn into bite-sized pieces

Bring a large pot of water to a boil. Generously salt the water and add the tortellini. Cook according to the package directions. Drain well. Drizzle with 1 tablespoon (15 ml) of olive oil, and gently toss to prevent sticking. Set aside.

In the meantime, turn the broiler to high. Add the asparagus to a baking sheet lined with parchment paper. Add 1 tablespoon (15 ml) of olive oil, massaging it evenly onto the asparagus spears. Season with salt and pepper.

Broil for approximately 10 minutes, turning the spears over halfway through, until the thickest part can be easily pierced with a fork. Keep a watchful eye though, as broiler temperatures vary. Set aside to cool. When cool to the touch, about 10 minutes, use a sharp knife to cut off the tips of each spear at the point where they meet the stem. Then, cut the stems into bite-sized pieces and divide them. Keep the tips and half of the stems in a separate bowl.

In a blender, add the remaining half of the roasted stems (about 3 oz [90 g]), the garlic, almonds, ⅓ cup (80 ml) of olive oil, Parmigiano, lemon juice and ¼ teaspoon of salt. Pulse until pureed. Set aside.

In a large serving bowl, combine the leafy greens, tortellini and the asparagus tips and stems that were set aside; toss together to mix. Add the desired amount of pesto, tossing to lightly coat, passing any leftover pesto at the table. Drizzle with more olive oil if necessary to loosen the pasta.

To serve, divide into individual serving bowls, drizzle with more olive oil and top with freshly ground pepper and grated cheese.

Cook's Notes: *Unsure where to trim off the ends on an asparagus spear? Gently bend it at the bottom. It will naturally break at the point where the tough stem meets the tender part.*

Strozzapreti with Peas, Pancetta and Red Dandelion Greens in Wine

Red dandelion greens are not dandelions at all—rather they are members of the chicory family. When tossed with hand-harvested spring peas and shallots and slightly wilted in white wine, their peppery bite is a splendid addition to pasta. Strozzapreti are medium-sized pastas with a unique shape, creating a delicate fold that cradles the essence of the wine and broth.

Serves 4–6

Kosher salt, as needed

1 lb (454 g) strozzapreti (substitute with gemelli)

2 tbsp (30 ml) extra-virgin olive oil, plus more for drizzling

4 oz (112 g) chopped pancetta

2 large shallots, roughly chopped

2 cups (110 g) red dandelion greens, roughly chopped, tough stems and unsightly leaves discarded

1 cup (240 ml) Sauvignon Blanc

1 cup (240 ml) chicken broth

1 cup (150 g) peas

¼ cup (25 g) freshly grated Parmigiano–Reggiano, plus more for garnish

Freshly ground pepper, to taste

Bring a large pot of water to a boil. Generously salt the water and add the pasta. Cook until just shy of al dente, tender yet firm to the bite, according to the package directions. Reserve ½ cup (120 ml) of the pasta water before draining. Drain well.

In the meantime, add the olive oil and the pancetta to a large 12-inch (30-cm) skillet with deep sides, over low–medium heat, tossing often until almost crisp, 5 to 6 minutes. Use a slotted spoon to transfer the pancetta to a paper towel–lined plate and set aside. Do not drain the olive oil from the skillet.

Add the chopped shallots to the skillet, then cook, stirring frequently, until the shallots begin to soften, 5 minutes. Add the dandelion greens and stir until they are wilted and the shallots are tender, 2 to 3 minutes more.

Remove the pan from the heat and slowly add the wine, taking care to not let it splatter, as the skillet is hot. Return the pan to the heat and scrape the bottom of the pan to deglaze any flavorful brown bits that may have accumulated. Add the broth and stir to combine. Bring the contents to a boil, then reduce to a simmer.

Add the pasta, ¼ cup (60 ml) of the reserved pasta water, peas and pancetta to the simmering wine and broth. Toss well to mix and to finish cooking the pasta, 1 minute. Turn off the heat.

Slowly add the grated Parmigiano while tossing to combine. Taste and adjust seasonings if necessary. If pasta appears too loose, continue to toss for another minute. Pasta will continue to thicken upon standing. Only use the remaining pasta water if the pasta absorbs too much liquid and needs to be loosened.

To serve, drizzle lightly with extra-virgin olive oil, freshly ground pepper and grated cheese.

Fiddlehead Pasta Primavera

Fiddleheads are the spiraled fronds of young ferns. The name "fiddlehead" comes from its resemblance to the scrolled top of the fiddle and violin. The name alone makes me seek these quirky little veggies out each spring. They add whimsy and charm to a simple pasta dish and are always a conversation piece at the table—especially when served to someone who is enjoying them for the first time. Fiddleheads are one of spring's elusive treats; they'll come and go in the blink of an eye, so act fast if you see them at the market. I like to pair fiddleheads with a fun curlicue pasta like campanelle.

Serves 4

6 oz (170 g) fresh fiddleheads

Kosher salt

12 oz (340 g) campanelle

2 tbsp (30 g) butter

¼ cup (60 ml) extra-virgin olive oil, plus more for drizzling

¼ tsp red pepper flakes

Freshly ground pepper

1 clove garlic, finely grated

1 cup (240 ml) chicken or vegetable broth

1 cup (30 g) packed arugula, stems cut and any unsightly leaves discarded

¼ cup (25 g) finely grated Parmigiano-Reggiano, plus more for serving

To clean the fiddleheads, fill a bowl with cold water (or use a salad spinner for ease, as the inner colander can be lifted to remove the fiddleheads from the dirty water), add the fiddleheads and swish them around to remove the dirt, keeping in mind to gently clean within the coils too. Trim the ends. Set aside.

Bring a large pot of water to a boil. Generously salt and add the pasta. Cook until just shy of al dente, tender yet firm to the bite, according to the package directions. Reserve ½ cup (120 ml) of the pasta water before draining. Drain well.

In the meantime, melt the butter and olive oil in a large 12-inch (30-cm) skillet over medium-high heat. When the butter begins to foam, add the fiddleheads, red pepper flakes and season to taste with salt and pepper. Cook, stirring gently and tossing to turn over every so often. Cook until the fiddleheads become crisp and tender and start to caramelize, 6 to 8 minutes.

Add the garlic to the skillet and sauté until fragrant, 30 seconds. Use a slotted spoon to remove the fiddleheads from the skillet and set aside.

Add the broth to the skillet and simmer to fully heat through, 2 to 3 minutes. Add the pasta, arugula and ¼ cup (60 ml) of the reserved pasta water. Toss well to incorporate, about 1 minute.

Slowly add the grated cheese, while tossing, to incorporate. If the pasta needs to be loosened, add the remaining reserved pasta water and a drizzle of olive oil. The pasta should be silky with a brothy essence, though not soupy. Add the fiddleheads back to the skillet and gently toss everything together.

To serve, garnish with a light drizzle of olive oil and more freshly grated cheese, passing more cheese at the table.

Cook's Notes: *Fiddleheads need to be thoroughly cooked. To be sure, you can blanch them in boiling water for 2 to 3 minutes before adding them to the hot skillet.*

Orzo with Crispy Scallions and Goat Cheese

When scallions start to fill the farm markets by the bundles, I'll always grab a handful or two. Scallions have a lot to offer a dish when thought of as more than just a garnish. When roasted, the white parts of the scallions soften, while retaining a subtle bite, and the dark green parts char and blister, adding another layer of flavor. Roasted scallions, when roughly chopped, add a distinct aromatic and visual element to a simple dish like orzo. A favorite side-dish pasta, orzo is reminiscent of a traditional rice pilaf and can be used in the same way. While this dish is perfectly comforting as a light lunch or served alongside a spring salad, consider tossing this together with salmon or grilled chicken to make a complete meal.

Serves 4–6

2 bunches scallions (about 7 oz [198 g] when trimmed)

4–5 tbsp (60–75 ml) extra-virgin olive oil, divided, plus more for drizzling

Kosher salt, to taste

1 lb (454 g) dry orzo

1 tbsp (15 g) butter, room temperature

Freshly ground pepper, to taste

Goat cheese crumbles, herbed or plain, for garnish

Clean the scallions well and pat them dry. Trim off the roots, peeling away any translucent, silvery husk (if necessary). Also trim away any unsightly parts on the darker green stems (usually just the tips need trimming) and arrange them on a baking sheet.

Massage the scallions well with 1 to 2 tablespoons (15 to 30 ml) of olive oil and a sprinkle of salt. Set the scallions under a broiler set to high. Broil for 3 to 5 minutes; scallions will cook quickly, so keep a watchful eye on them. If the scallions are rather large, you might need to flip them over to broil the other side. They will begin to char and blister in some spots while retaining their soft bite in other places. Remove the scallions from the broiler and set aside. Once cool to the touch, give them a rough chop; because the white parts are more substantial, chop them a bit finer.

In the meantime, bring a large pot of water to a boil. Generously salt the water and add the orzo. Cook until al dente, tender yet firm to the bite, according to the package directions. Reserve ½ cup (120 ml) of the pasta water before draining. Drain well. Drizzle the orzo with 3 tablespoons (45 ml) of olive oil and add the butter and ¼ cup (60 ml) of the reserved pasta water. Season to taste with salt and pepper.

Reserve some of the charred scallions for garnish. Add the rest of the scallions to the orzo, tossing well to combine and melt the butter.

To serve, divide into individual serving bowls and top with the desired amount of crumbled goat cheese and a light drizzle of olive oil.

Cook's Notes: *Get creative! Toss in leftover asparagus, peas or mushrooms. Mix up the flavor combinations by garnishing with fresh ribbons of Parmigiano-Reggiano instead of goat cheese. This recipe will flow into summer beautifully with the addition of roasted corn and peppers or other seasonal favorites.*

Pappardelle with Artichokes, Spinach and Goat Cheese

This dish reflects the tenderness of the new season. I've used delicate baby spinach, newly harvested baby artichokes and ribbons of pappardelle. Everything comes together when the pasta warms the goat cheese until just barely melting.

Serves 4

2 lemons, halved

6-7 fresh baby artichokes

¼ cup (60 ml) extra-virgin olive oil, plus more for drizzling

¼ tsp red pepper flakes

1 small onion, finely chopped

Kosher salt, as needed

12 oz (340 g) pappardelle

2 cups (60 g) packed, fresh baby spinach, rinsed

2 cloves garlic, finely grated

1 cup (240 ml) white wine

½ cup (120 ml) chicken broth

Freshly ground pepper, to taste

½ cup (115 g) crumbled goat cheese, plus more for serving

To prepare the artichokes, fill a large bowl with water, squeeze the juice from one lemon into the water and drop the squeezed halves into the bowl. Working with one artichoke at a time, use a serrated knife to cut off the spiky top fourth of the artichoke. Use the cut halves of the other lemon to rub onto the cut and exposed parts of the artichoke to prevent oxidation. Pull back and peel off the dark green outer leaves until you reach the pale green and yellow layer. Trim the bottom of the stem with a sharp knife and use a vegetable peeler to peel and smooth out the stem. Discard the trimmings. Halve or quarter the artichokes lengthwise, depending on the size. Use the lemon again to rub onto the cut parts. If the choke looks spiky, remove it. Otherwise the choke on baby artichokes is perfectly edible. Drop the trimmed artichoke into the bowl of lemon water. Repeat with the remaining artichokes.

In a 12-inch (30-cm) deep skillet, heat the olive oil over low-medium heat. When it is hot and shimmery, add the red pepper flakes and onion, sprinkle lightly with salt and cook, stirring often, until softened, 8 to 10 minutes.

Meanwhile, bring a large pot of water to a boil. Generously salt the water and add the pasta. Cook until just shy of al dente, tender yet firm to the bite, according to the package directions. Add the spinach to the pasta water during the last minute of cooking. Reserve 1 cup (240 ml) of the pasta water before draining. Drain well.

Add the garlic to the skillet, stirring until fragrant, about 30 seconds, taking care not to burn. Remove the skillet from the heat to add the wine, then return the skillet to medium heat and add the broth. Let the mixture come to a simmer, about 1 minute.

Drain the artichokes from the lemon water and discard the lemon halves. Add the artichokes to the skillet, cover and cook, stirring occasionally, until tender, 15 minutes. Give the artichokes a taste and check for tenderness before adding the pasta. The thickest part of the artichoke should be easily pierced with a fork and the leaves and stem should be tender; if not, cook a few minutes longer. Season to taste with salt and pepper.

Add the spinach and pasta to the artichokes in the skillet and gently toss to combine. Add half of the goat cheese and ¼ cup (60 ml) of the reserved pasta water and toss together gently. If the pasta needs to be loosened, add more of the reserved pasta water, a little at a time.

Serve hot with a drizzle of olive oil and the remaining goat cheese.

Spaghetti alla Chitarra with Braised Leeks and Wine

The leeks that slept through winter, protected under mounds of soil and mulch in the deep, cold fields, emerge in the springtime full of sweet earthiness. Braised leeks impart a subtle, yet distinct, flavor that is perfect for a starring role in this quick springtime pasta dish.

Serves 4

6 medium-sized leeks, ends trimmed, white and pale green parts only, thinly sliced lengthwise

4 tbsp (60 g) butter

2 tbsp (30 ml) extra-virgin olive oil, plus more for drizzling

2 shallots, sliced thin

Kosher salt

12 oz (340 g) spaghetti alla chitarra (can substitute with any long pasta)

½ cup (120 ml) Sauvignon Blanc

1 cup (240 ml) chicken broth

¼ cup (60 ml) heavy cream

Freshly ground black pepper

Grated Parmigiano-Reggiano or local cheese with a hard and sharp profile, to taste

Place the cut leeks in a large bowl of cold water. Swish them around with your hands to help separate the layers and release the dirt. Then let them soak in the water for approximately 5 minutes. The leeks will float to the top of the water and the dirt will fall to the bottom (using a salad spinner with the interior colander is a helpful tool to soak and lift the leeks out of the water). After soaking, remove the leeks and discard the dirty water. Give the leeks a final rinse in a colander under running water, shaking out as much excess water as possible.

Add the butter and the olive oil to a 12-inch (30-cm) skillet with deep sides, over medium heat. When the oil is hot and the butter is melted, add the shallots and leeks. Season with salt and cook, stirring and gently folding over occasionally, until the leeks are tender, have significantly softened and are lightly browned, 30 to 35 minutes (the leeks will become easier to stir as they gradually soften).

While the leeks braise, bring a large pot of water to a boil. Generously salt the water and add the pasta. Cook until just shy of al dente, tender but firm to the bite, according to the package directions. Reserve ½ cup (120 ml) of the pasta water before draining. Drain well.

When the leeks have braised, remove the skillet from the heat to add the wine, scraping the bottom of the pan to loosen any flavorful brown bits that have formed there. Return the pan to low heat and simmer for 1 minute more. Add the broth and heavy cream, then simmer for another minute to thicken the sauce. Sprinkle with freshly ground black pepper to desired taste and toss gently to combine.

Add the pasta to the skillet along with ¼ cup (60 ml) of the reserved pasta water, toss together to combine and until some of the liquid has been absorbed, about 1 minute. If necessary, add more pasta water and add a generous drizzle of olive oil to loosen the pasta, tossing to combine.

To serve, drizzle lightly with olive oil and add a generous amount of freshly grated cheese.

Cook's Notes: *Leeks are dirty! Fan the cut leeks under running cool water to release any surface dirt and help facilitate cleaning before plunging in a bowl of cold water. The tough green portion of the leeks could be saved to flavor soups, though you'll need to discard after use.*

Bucatini with Rapini in Pepper Oil

Rapini, often referred to as broccoli rabe, is not related to broccoli at all. In fact, it's a relative of the turnip family. What I love most about rapini though is the way its tender, delicate broccoli-esque buds sit tucked in among the leafy greens, like little bouquets. That's enough to make me want to buy them! Here I've paired them with the deep flavor of anchovy and the subtle crunch of breadcrumbs for texture. Red pepper flakes toast in extra-virgin olive oil to create the perfect infused oil to dress up and coat plump and tender strands of bucatini.

Serves 4–6

2 tbsp (30 ml) plus ½ cup (120 ml) extra-virgin olive oil, divided

⅔ cup (60 g) fine breadcrumbs

Kosher salt and freshly ground pepper

1 tsp red pepper flakes

5 anchovy fillets, packed in oil

1 clove garlic, finely grated

1 lb (454 g) bucatini

8 oz (227 g or about half of a bunch) rapini, rinsed, thick stems trimmed and leaves roughly chopped

Grated Parmigiano-Reggiano or local cheese with a hard and sharp profile, to garnish

In a medium skillet over low-medium heat, add 2 tablespoons (30 ml) of olive oil and the breadcrumbs and mix well, stirring and pressing down, until all the oil is absorbed; it will take a minute or two for it to come together and resemble coarse wet sand. At that point, spread the breadcrumbs evenly to let them darken and toast, stirring often, 5 minutes. Don't be afraid to let them darken, just take care not to burn. If using unseasoned breadcrumbs, lightly season with salt and freshly ground pepper, then remove from the heat and set aside.

In a separate large 12-inch (30-cm) skillet over low-medium heat, add ½ cup (120 ml) of olive oil. When the oil is hot and shimmery, add the red pepper flakes and anchovies. Cook, stirring frequently, until the anchovies nearly disintegrate and the red pepper flakes have toasted and infused the oil, about 5 minutes. Turn off the heat. Add the garlic. The heat from the oil will soften the garlic immediately.

Meanwhile, bring a large pot of water to a boil. Generously salt the water and add the pasta. Cook until a minute or two shy of al dente, tender yet firm to the bite, according to the package directions. Add the rapini to the boiling water during the last minute of cooking. It will take just about that time for the rapini to become bright green and tender. Reserve 1 cup (240 ml) of the cooking water before draining. Drain well.

Add the pasta, rapini and ¼ cup (60 ml) of the reserved pasta water to the skillet with the oil. Turn the heat under the skillet to low-medium and toss frequently to combine the flavors and to finish cooking the pasta, 1 to 2 minutes. Continue to add more pasta water, a little at a time, if needed to loosen the pasta. The consistency should be silky, not pasty or sticky.

To serve, divide the pasta into individual bowls and top with the desired amount of toasted breadcrumbs, passing the rest at the table, along with freshly grated cheese.

Cacio e Pepe with Fava (Broad) Beans

Cacio e pepe literally means "cheese and pepper." Each bite of this dish is threaded with memories of my grandmother lifting long creamy strands of piping hot linguine and nestling them onto a plate, swirling them into a heap and topping with specks of cracked black pepper and ribbons of freshly grated pecorino. I'll warn you though, this is one of those dishes that people will argue about—purists will say never add butter and only use pecorino. Others will say olive oil is fine and Parmigiano-Reggiano is a good substitute. That's the beauty of cooking though—everyone is right in their own kitchen, even if their version deviates a little from tradition. I toss in fava beans in the spring with their ancient, old-world flavor and buttery texture. Since the rest of the dish comes together so quickly, the little effort needed to shell the beans is well worth the time.

Serves 4–6

Kosher salt, to taste

1 lb (454 g) fava or broad beans (to equal about ½ cup [130 g] when peeled) or substitute with dry beans

1 lb (454 g) linguine (substitute with any long, thick pasta)

1½ tsp (5 g) coarsely ground pepper

6 tbsp (90 g) salted butter, cubed

¼ cup (60 ml) extra-virgin olive oil

1 cup (180 g) grated Pecorino Romano, plus more to garnish

Bring a medium pot of salted water to a boil to blanch the beans. Keep an ice bath (a bowl with cold water and ice) next to the stove.

Blanch the beans in the salted boiling water for 1 minute, drain and then plunge the beans into the ice bath to stop the cooking, about 1 minute. Drain the ice water, then pinch off and discard the outer skins of the beans. Set the beans aside.

Bring another large pot of water to a boil. Generously salt and add the pasta. Cook until just shy of al dente, tender yet firm to the bite, according to the package directions. Reserve at least 3 cups (720 ml) of the pasta water before draining. Drain well.

Meanwhile, to a large 12-inch (30-cm) skillet with deep sides over low–medium heat, add the coarsely ground pepper and a pinch of salt and let it toast, 1 minute. Slowly add 1 cup (240 ml) of the pasta water to the hot skillet, being careful as it may splatter at first, and stir.

Add the butter and olive oil and stir to emulsify, then add the pasta and the beans. Toss to coat the pasta well and to allow it to absorb some of the liquid, about 1 minute. Remove the skillet from the heat, add another ¼ cup (60 ml) of pasta water and continue to toss. Working quickly and constantly, continue to toss the pasta while slowly adding the cheese. Continue to toss for 1 to 2 minutes; this will ensure the pasta finishes cooking and the cheese melts evenly and sticks to the pasta and not to the bottom of the pan. If needed, add more pasta water, ¼ cup (60 ml) at a time, while continuing to toss until the desired consistency is reached, which should be silky and creamy. The pasta will continue to thicken upon standing.

Taste and adjust the seasonings—you'll want to taste the heat from the pepper, though it shouldn't be overwhelming. Serve hot with more freshly grated pecorino.

Cook's Notes: *If substituting with dried beans, note that they tend to be pre-blanched and are usually already shelled. Please refer to the package instructions to cook.*

Spring Spinach Mac and Cheese

Homemade macaroni and cheese ranks high on my list of comfort foods. With an abundance of farm-fresh baby spinach on hand, I toss a few handfuls into this dish for good springtime measure. Pancetta provides the perfect dose of savory while the melted fontina and mozzarella make it every bit as indulgent as a mac and cheese should be. This dish pairs wonderfully with a fresh spinach salad.

Serves 4–6, or 8–10 as a side dish

4 tbsp (60 g) butter, plus more to grease the baking dish

½ cup (45 g) fine Italian seasoned breadcrumbs

3 tbsp (15 g) grated Parmigiano–Reggiano cheese

3 tbsp (45 ml) extra-virgin olive oil, divided, plus more if needed

Kosher salt

1 lb (454 g) elbow macaroni

2 large shallots, roughly chopped

4 oz (112 g) chopped pancetta

1 cup (240 ml) Sauvignon Blanc or other dry white wine

2 cups (480 ml) light cream

4 tbsp (31 g) all-purpose, unbleached flour

Freshly ground pepper

1 cup (108 g) shredded fontina

2 cups (60 g) packed fresh spinach, roughly chopped

¾ cup (84 g) grated, packed mozzarella cheese

Lightly butter the bottom and sides of a 9 x 13-inch (23 x 33-cm) oven-proof baking dish and set aside. In a medium-sized bowl, mix the breadcrumbs, Parmigiano cheese and 1 tablespoon (15 ml) of the olive oil along with a sprinkle of salt. Mix well, pressing down to help the breadcrumbs absorb the olive oil, until the mixture resembles coarse wet sand. If more olive oil is needed, add an extra ½ teaspoon. Set aside.

Bring a large pot of water to a boil, generously salt and add the pasta. Cook until about 2 minutes shy of al dente, tender yet firm to the bite, according to the package directions. Reserve ½ cup (120 ml) of the pasta water before draining. Drain well.

In the meantime, in a large 12-inch (30-cm) skillet, heat 2 tablespoons (30 ml) of the olive oil. When the oil is hot and shimmery, add the shallots. Cook over low–medium heat, stirring often, until the shallots are almost tender, 5 minutes. Add the pancetta and cook until it is beginning to crisp and the shallots have fully softened, 5 minutes.

Remove the skillet from the heat and add the white wine. Return to low–medium heat and scrape the bottom of the pan to deglaze any flavorful brown bits that may have accumulated. Simmer the wine for 2 minutes. Lower the heat and add the cream. Add the butter and wait for it to melt thoroughly. Add the flour, whisking continuously to avoid lumps, season with salt and pepper to taste and simmer for 2 to 3 minutes more until the sauce has thickened enough to coat the back of a spoon. Stir in the fontina cheese and spinach until the cheese melts and the spinach is wilted. Season to taste with salt and pepper.

Add the pasta and the reserved pasta water to the baking dish. Stir in the spinach and fontina mixture and gently fold into the pasta, mixing to combine. Sprinkle the top with mozzarella cheese and a layer of the breadcrumb mixture. Place the baking dish under the broiler, set to high and bake until the breadcrumbs are lightly browned and toasted, about 2 minutes, keeping a watchful eye so the breadcrumbs don't burn. Serve hot or at room temperature. The pasta will thicken upon standing.

Toscani with Sautéed Radish Greens

Just-plucked radishes, still damp with earth and rain, have begun to grace the farm stands in abundance. I tend to buy several bunches at a time, especially when their green leaves are full and vibrant. If you've never enjoyed radish greens before, they offer a delicious peppery bite that pairs gorgeously with pasta. Buying or growing radishes is like two for the price of one! After you've separated the greens from their roots, wash and store the leaves like you would any other leafy green and enjoy them within a day or two. This is a fuss-free and simple spring dish that makes for a light lunch or dinner when served alongside a radish salad or as a side to your favorite main course.

Serves 4

10 oz (280 g) radish greens, discarding any unsightly or wilted leaves (from about 2 bunches)

Kosher salt

13 oz (368 g) toscani pasta (or any medium-sized pasta of choice)

¼ cup (60 ml) extra-virgin olive oil, plus more for drizzling

¼ tsp red pepper flakes

1 clove garlic, finely grated

Freshly ground pepper, to taste

Grated local cheese with a hard and sharp profile or Parmigiano-Reggiano, for serving

Wash the radish greens thoroughly, removing all traces of dirt, and lightly pat dry. Give the leaves a rough chop to create bite-sized pieces.

Bring a large pot of water to a boil. Generously salt the water and add the pasta. Cook until just shy of al dente, tender yet firm to the bite, according to the package directions. Reserve 1 cup (240 ml) of the pasta water before draining. Drain well.

In a large 12-inch (30-cm) skillet over low–medium heat, add the olive oil. When the oil is hot and shimmery, add the red pepper flakes, leaving them to toast, about 1 minute. Add the radish greens and stir until they have somewhat wilted and turned a darker shade of green, approximately 2 minutes. Add the garlic, cooking until fragrant, 30 seconds.

Add the pasta and ¼ cup (60 ml) of the reserved pasta water to the skillet. Gently toss to combine the flavors and to finish cooking the pasta, 1 to 2 minutes. Only add more pasta water to loosen the pasta if necessary. The pasta should be silky.

To serve, top with a drizzle of olive oil, freshly ground pepper and grated cheese.

Pasta with Fresh Ricotta, Peas and Mint

This recipe is the perfect example of why pasta shapes matter. Mezzi rigatoni, or any tubular or cupped-shaped pasta, will provide the perfect component for homemade ricotta cheese and freshly harvested peas to tuck inside with every bite. A light garnish of freshly-snipped mint adds just the right amount of bright spring flavor. If fresh ricotta is made in advance, the rest of this dish will come together in just one pot.

Serves 4–6

Kosher salt

1 lb (454 g) mezzi rigatoni (orecchiette or medium shells would work too)

1 cup (150 g) fresh peas (can substitute with frozen)

¼ cup (60 g) butter, room temperature

¼ cup (25 g) finely grated Parmigiano–Reggiano, plus additional for serving

Juice of one medium lemon

¼ cup (60 ml) extra-virgin olive oil, plus more as needed

Freshly ground pepper, to taste

1 cup (246 g) fresh ricotta cheese (page 34) or good-quality store-bought

Fresh mint, cut in slivers, to garnish

Bring a large pot of water to a boil. Generously salt the water and add the pasta. Cook until just shy of al dente, tender yet firm to the bite, according to the package directions. Add the peas to the pot of boiling water in the last minute of cooking. Reserve 1 cup (240 ml) of the pasta water before draining. Drain well and return the pasta and peas to the pot. Lower the heat to a simmer.

Add the butter and the reserved pasta water to the pot and begin to toss while adding the grated Parmigiano, a little at a time, to ensure an even melt and to prevent the cheese from sticking to the bottom of the pot.

Add the lemon juice and olive oil, and stir well to combine. Taste. The essence should be bright and lemony. If the lemon makes you pucker, add a little more olive oil to balance the acidity. Season with salt and a few turns of coarsely ground black pepper, gently mixing to combine. Transfer to a serving bowl.

Dollop the ricotta cheese on top of the pasta and lightly fold together once or twice—the idea is to leave the ricotta somewhat in dollops.

To serve, divide into individual servings and lightly drizzle with olive oil, more grated cheese and slivers of fresh mint.

Spinach and Avocado Linguine

I recently discovered how delicately creamy and light a piping hot bowl of silky linguine could taste when cloaked in a raw spinach and avocado dressing. This meal is quick and easy and ready in the time it takes to boil water. The dressing is pureed and added raw, warmed only by the heat from the tendrils of linguine. A handful of fresh baby spinach imparts a delicate greenish hue that is perfect for a springtime pasta dish. A squeeze of lemon brightens the flavors and brings it all together. Consider adding shrimp, salmon, grilled chicken or, as one recipe tester suggested, red pepper flakes for heat— or simply enjoy as is, preferably al fresco, on a late afternoon.

Serves 4–6

¼ tsp kosher salt, plus more for cooking pasta

1 lb (454 g) linguine

2 ripe medium avocados, pitted

1 cup (30 g) lightly packed fresh spinach leaves

¼ cup (25 g) grated local cheese with a hard and sharp profile or Parmigiano–Reggiano, plus more to garnish

1 clove garlic, smashed

1 tsp fresh thyme, center stem discarded

1–4 tbsp (15–60 ml) freshly squeezed lemon juice, depending on preference

2 tbsp (30 ml) extra-virgin olive oil, plus more for drizzling

Coarsely ground fresh pepper, to taste

Bring a large pot of water to a boil. Generously salt the water and add the pasta. Cook until al dente, tender yet firm to the bite, according to the package directions. Reserve 2 cups (480 ml) of the pasta water before draining. Drain well.

In the meantime, scoop the flesh from the ripe avocados, discarding the skins and pits. In a high-powered food processor, combine the avocados, spinach, grated cheese, garlic and thyme. Add the desired amount of lemon juice. If you are unsure about the amount to use, start by adding only 1 tablespoon (15 ml) and proceed with the recipe, then taste after the sauce has been added to the pasta—you can always add more lemon juice; giving a gentle toss, before serving.

Add the olive oil and kosher salt to the food processor and pulse until smooth and creamy, scraping down the sides of the processor if needed. The texture should be creamy. If the sauce appears a bit thick, you can thin it a bit later with pasta water. Set the mixture aside.

Add the pasta to a large serving bowl. Add the avocado mixture and ½ cup (120 ml) of the reserved pasta water, tossing well to coat, about 1 minute. Continue to add more pasta water, a little at a time, tossing well with each addition of water, until the desired consistency is reached. The final texture should be creamy with movement.

To serve, top with freshly grated cheese, coarsely ground fresh pepper and a light drizzle of olive oil.

Cook's Notes: *Avocado tends to oxidize, turning brown, once cut. While the citric acid of the lemon juice will slow this process, the dressing will begin to slightly discolor over time. This dish is best served the same day it is prepared.*

Spring Pasta with Arugula and Strawberries

When pasta is used as a supporting ingredient, it allows the unexpected pairing of ripe strawberries to take the lead. When combined with the sharp bite of a creamy blue cheese crumble, a good measure of peppery arugula and a balsamic reduction, you'll have a wonderfully sweet and savory option to celebrate the strawberry harvest.

Serves 4

Kosher salt, to taste

12 oz (340 g) farfalle

¼ cup (60 ml) extra-virgin olive oil

½ cup (120 ml) balsamic vinegar

½ cup (68 g) crumbled blue cheese, plus more for serving

4 cups (120 g) mixed fresh arugula and/or baby spinach (or preferred amount)

Freshly ground pepper, to taste

2 cups (302 g) strawberries, hulled and quartered

Bring a large pot of water to a boil. Generously salt the water and add the pasta. Cook until al dente, tender yet firm to the bite, according to the package directions. Briefly rinse the pasta under cool water to stop the cooking and remove some of the starch. Drain well. Transfer the pasta to a large serving bowl. Add the olive oil and toss well to combine. Set aside.

Meanwhile, in a small saucepan over high heat, add the balsamic vinegar and bring it to a boil. Reduce the heat to low and simmer for approximately 15 minutes, or until it is reduced by half and syrupy—don't overcook it though or it will harden like candy upon cooling; you'll want the vinegar to be thick enough to coat the back of a spoon but remain pourable.

Add the blue cheese and arugula to the pasta, then gently toss to combine. Season with salt and pepper, to taste, and toss again.

Add the strawberries last and gently toss—too much tossing will stain the pasta pink and compromise the strawberries if they're very ripe. Alternatively, you can use the strawberries as a generous garnish for each serving.

To serve, drizzle the pasta lightly with the balsamic glaze, passing the rest at the table. Garnish with extra blue cheese crumbles.

Fresh Spinach Fettuccine Carbonara

This is the bacon and eggs of pasta. Taking the time to prepare fresh pasta is always a treat and it never disappoints. Adding fresh spring spinach to homemade pasta dough elevates this dish to a whole other level and adding more baby spinach to a simple carbonara adds bright seasonal color and subtle earthy flavor. This is my absolute favorite pasta recipe to make when the spinach harvest is abundant. Be sure to serve with rustic, crusty bread to mop up of all that fragrant and creamy sauce!

Serves 4—6

1 cup (30 g) plus 3 oz (90 g) packed fresh baby spinach, rinsed

Fresh Pasta Dough (page 16)

2 tbsp (30 ml) extra-virgin olive oil

4 oz (112 g) pancetta or guanciale (salt-cured pork jowl), roughly chopped

2 medium cloves garlic, finely grated

Kosher salt, as needed

3 large egg yolks, room temperature

1 cup (150 g) grated Parmigiano-Reggiano, plus more to garnish

¼ tsp coarsely ground pepper, plus more to garnish

Wash 1 cup (30 g) of the spinach and drain it briefly. Toss it damp into a hot, dry skillet to wilt, 2 to 3 minutes. Have a bowl of ice water near the stove. When the spinach is wilted, remove it from the skillet and plunge it into the ice bath. Allow the spinach to cool, about 2 minutes. Drain very well. Use paper towels to wring out the excess water or press into a sieve to remove as much moisture as possible. Finely chop the spinach and add it to the egg mixture as directed in the Basic Pasta Dough recipe (page 16). Proceed with the directions there for kneading, rolling and cutting the dough into fettuccine.

In a large 12-inch (30-cm) skillet with deep sides over low–medium heat, add the olive oil and pancetta and cook, tossing often, until the pancetta is crisp, 5 to 6 minutes. Remove the skillet from the heat and add the garlic, stirring to combine. Set the skillet aside. The garlic will become fragrant and soften in the hot oil almost immediately.

Bring a large pot of water to a boil. Generously salt the water and add the pasta. Cook the pasta, noting that fresh pasta cooks quickly, usually in 1 to 2 minutes. Add 3 oz (90 g) fresh spinach directly to the boiling water at the end of cooking. The hot pasta water will wilt the spinach perfectly. Reserve 2 cups (480 ml) of the pasta water before draining. Drain well.

Meanwhile, in a medium bowl, beat the egg yolks. Very slowly add 1 cup (240 ml) of the reserved pasta water into the egg mixture in a steady stream while whisking quickly to temper and to avoid scrambling the eggs. Add the grated cheese, lightly season with salt and coarsely ground pepper and whisk again until well incorporated and as smooth as possible, paying mind to any large clumps of cheese. This will create a silky sauce for the pasta.

Set a low heat under the skillet with the pancetta and garlic and add the hot fettuccine and spinach. Slowly pour in the egg mixture while continuously tossing the pasta, 1 to 2 minutes, to help the sauce absorb into the pasta and thicken up. The sauce should be creamy, and the pasta should not be pasty. Only add more reserved pasta water, a little at a time, to loosen the pasta if necessary (keep any remaining water on hand, if needed, until the meal is done). The sauce will continue to thicken as it sits. Serve immediately. Pass extra grated cheese and ground pepper at the table.

Cook's Notes: *It is important to cook the fettuccine while preparing the sauce. It is the heat from the fettuccine that will fully cook the egg mixture and will create a silky sauce that sticks to the pasta.*

Tuscan Hand-Rolled Pici with Lamb Ragu and Mint

Pici pasta is one of my most favorite homemade pastas to make for its rustic beauty. While it resembles a plumped-up version of spaghetti, it's the history behind pici that I appreciate most. The old-world Tuscan peasants, like so many others, could make something beautiful from almost nothing at all. Pici was created when ingredients were scarce—when there was only a little flour in the cupboard and water on hand. It's an eggless pasta that is hand rolled, so no pasta machine is required. This pasta pairs beautifully with the earthy flavor of ground lamb and hints of fresh spring mint.

Serves 4–6

Fresh Pici

1¼ cups (219 g) semolina flour, plus more for dusting

1¾ cups (219 g) all-purpose flour, or more as needed

2 tbsp (30 ml) extra-virgin olive oil

1 cup (240 ml) water

To make the pici, mix the two flours together with a fork until well incorporated. This process is the same as making standard dough, only without the use of eggs. I prefer to mix by using the well method, wherein the flour is added to the work surface in a mound. Make a hole in the center and add the olive oil and water. Follow the Basic Pasta Dough recipe (page 16) , only for mixing and kneading; once the dough has been kneaded and has rested, proceed as below.

With a sharp knife, divide the dough in half, leaving one half wrapped in plastic wrap. Using a rolling pin, roll out the dough onto a lightly floured work surface until it is about ¼ inch (6 mm) thick. Use a sharp knife to cut the dough into lengthwise strips.

Taking one strip at a time, begin to roll out the piece of dough with your fingers, starting in the middle and working toward the outside. Essentially you will be making a rope shape, about ¼ inch (6 mm) thick. The length should be about 6 inches (15 cm), so if you have made a very long rope, simply use a sharp knife to cut it back.

The noodles should be thicker than spaghetti but not as thick as a pencil. Uneven and varying degrees of thickness and length make this pasta beautifully rustic, so don't worry too much about having the perfect shape.

Place the rolled noodles on a semolina-dusted surface until ready to use.

Bring a large pot of water to a boil.

(continued)

Tuscan Hand-Rolled Pici with Lamb Ragu and Mint (Continued)

Sauce

¼ cup (60 ml) extra-virgin olive oil, plus more for drizzling

1 tbsp (15 g) butter

1 large onion, finely chopped

Kosher salt, to taste

2 medium cloves garlic, finely grated

4 oz (112 g) chopped pancetta

1 lb (454 g) ground lamb

6 oz (170 g) tomato paste

1 cup (240 ml) dry red wine

1 (28-oz [794-g]) can whole, peeled San Marzano tomatoes, roughly crushed and juices reserved

1 cup (240 ml) low-sodium chicken broth

2 bay leaves

Freshly ground pepper, to taste

1 lb (454 g) fresh pici

Fresh mint, slivered, to garnish

Grated local cheese with a hard and sharp profile or Parmigiano–Reggiano, to garnish

In the meantime, over low–medium heat, add the olive oil and butter to a large 13- to 15-inch (33- to 38-cm) skillet with deep sides or a Dutch oven. When the oil is hot and shimmery and the butter is melted, add the onion and lightly sprinkle with salt. Cook, stirring often, until the onion is soft and beginning to caramelize, about 10 minutes. Add the garlic and sauté until fragrant, 30 seconds.

Add the pancetta and lamb over moderate heat, stirring often, about 10 minutes.

Make a "hot spot" in the pot by pushing the lamb and pancetta to the sides to expose the hot center of the pan, then add the tomato paste to the center. Stir the paste briefly, and then let it sit in the hot spot for a few minutes to caramelize, 2 to 3 minutes. Stir to combine the paste with the lamb and pancetta mixture.

Remove the pot from the heat to add the wine, then stir to combine. Return to moderate heat and scrape the bottom of the pan to deglaze any flavorful brown bits that may have accumulated. Cook until the wine is reduced by half, 5 minutes.

Add the tomatoes (with their juice), broth and bay leaves. Season with salt and pepper and bring the contents to a boil. Reduce the heat to a simmer, stirring often, until the lamb is tender and fully cooked through, 10 minutes. Discard the bay leaves. Turn off the heat and cover while waiting for the pasta.

Generously salt the boiling water and add the fresh pici. Note that fresh pasta will cook faster than dried, usually within 1 to 2 minutes. Reserve ¼ cup (60 ml) of the pasta water before draining. Drain well.

Add a low heat under the skillet and add the pasta and the reserved pasta water to the lamb mixture, stirring well to combine. To serve, garnish with the desired amount of slivered fresh mint, a drizzle of olive oil and grated cheese.

Garganelli (Handmade Penne) with Baby Artichokes and Garlic Butter

When I was growing up, my grandmother would steam artichokes for me and my little brothers, and we would devour them by dipping the ends of the meaty leaves into a simple mixture of melted butter, lemon and garlic. For ease of convenience, I've used baby artichokes in this dish. If you've never made homemade penne before, give it a go; it's much easier than you'd think, and the hollows of the fresh pasta will fill with the flavorful essence of wine and broth. Prepare the fresh pasta ahead of time to save on recipe preparation.

Serves 4–6

Basic Pasta Dough recipe (page 16)

2 lemons, halved, plus 2–3 tbsp (30–45 ml) fresh squeezed lemon juice

6–8 baby artichokes (substitute with canned or jarred artichoke hearts packed in water)

¼ cup (60 ml) extra-virgin olive oil

3 small cloves garlic, finely grated, setting one aside to garnish

1 cup (240 ml) Sauvignon Blanc

½ cup (120 ml) chicken broth

Kosher salt and freshly ground pepper, to taste

4 tbsp (60 g) butter, melted

Prepare the fresh penne by following the ingredients and directions set forth in the Basic Pasta Dough recipe (page 16). After the dough has been kneaded, rolled out and is ready to be shaped, proceed as follows.

Working with 1½-inch (3.7-cm) squares of rolled pasta, lay a square diagonally in front of you. Wrap one corner of the square around a clean candy apple stick, pen or pencil. Using gentle pressure, push the dough away from you until the pasta is completely wrapped around the stick. Slide the shaped pasta off the stick and repeat. Lay the shaped pasta on a floured surface to dry.

To prepare the artichokes, fill a large bowl with water, squeeze the juice from one lemon into the water and drop the squeezed halves into the bowl. Working with one artichoke at a time, use a serrated knife to cut off the spiky top quarter of the artichoke. Use the cut halves of the other lemon to rub onto the cut and exposed parts of the artichoke to prevent oxidation. Pull back and peel off the dark green outer leaves until you reach the pale green and yellow layer. Trim the bottom of the stem with a sharp knife and use a vegetable peeler to peel and smooth out the stem; discard the trimmings. Halve or quarter the artichokes lengthwise, depending on the size. Use the lemon again to rub onto the cut parts. If the choke looks spiky, remove it. Otherwise the choke on baby artichokes is perfectly edible. Drop the artichoke into the bowl of lemon water. Repeat with the remaining artichokes.

(continued)

Garganelli (Handmade Penne) with Baby Artichokes and Garlic Butter (Continued)

Add the olive oil to a large 12-inch (30-cm) skillet, over low-medium heat. When the oil is hot and shimmery, add two of the grated garlic cloves, stirring until fragrant, about 30 seconds, and being careful not to let it burn.

Remove the skillet from the heat and carefully add the wine. Return the pan to moderate heat, and bring the wine to a low boil to allow it to reduce a bit, 3 minutes. Add the broth and the artichokes to the skillet and lightly season to taste with salt and pepper. Cover and cook until the artichokes are tender, 15 to 20 minutes or until the thickest part of the artichoke can be easily pierced with a fork and the leaves are tender. If using jarred artichoke hearts, halve them and cook until heated through, 3 minutes.

Meanwhile, bring a large pot of water to a boil. Generously salt the water and add the pasta. Keep a watchful eye as fresh pasta cooks more quickly than dry, usually in 1 to 2 minutes. Reserve ½ cup (120 ml) of the pasta water before draining. Drain well.

Add the pasta and ¼ cup (60 ml) of the reserved pasta water to the skillet and gently toss to combine. Taste and adjust the seasonings. If necessary, add more of the reserved water to loosen the pasta. The consistency should be fluid and have movement.

In a small bowl, combine the melted butter, lemon juice and the last grated garlic clove; stir the ingredients together. Drizzle the desired amount of the lemon–butter–garlic mixture lightly over each serving of pasta, passing any leftover mixture at the table. Garnish with freshly ground pepper.

Cook's Notes: *To add some color to this dish, consider adding fresh peas and a garnish of fresh thyme if it's in season.*

"It's a comfort to always find pasta in the cupboard and garlic and parsley in the garden."
—Alice Waters

SUMMER

Oh, summer! The late afternoon sun intensifies the aroma of fresh earth and grass and the nights are aglow with a thousand fireflies. The harvest is abundant at our local farm market, Donaldson Farms, and we wait with anticipation for their "Our Own Corn" sign on the side of the road. While raw and straight off the cob is the most divine way to enjoy their corn, we still find many ways to include it in our summer dishes, like in Blueberry and Raw Sweet Corn Orzo with Basil and Thyme (page 143).

The summer earth provides such robust colors, too. Ruby-red beets still caked with damp earth are among my favorites of the vibrant season, and they provide for us twice—not only with their colorful bulbs but with their leafy greens, too. Look for a bunch with large, unwilted leaves, and it will doubly reward you in the kitchen. If you'd like to try your hand at a colorful fresh pasta while you're at it, a little beet puree will yield beautiful, silky crimson noodles in my Fresh Beetroot Pasta with Lemon Basil and Beet Greens (page 175).

The unwavering heat of summer calls for less time at the stove and for dinner to be enjoyed outdoors after the blazing sun has set, so we oblige Mother Nature with cold pasta salads and with more raw ingredients straight from the garden or field. Take a peek at my Cucumber Pasta Salad with Creamy Dill (page 167), Tortellini Summer Salad with Basil Vinaigrette (page 171) or Penne Lisce with Blackberries, Balsamic and Basil (page 144), just to name a few.

Tomatoes are the quintessential summer staple. As summer continues to unfold, plump tomatoes overcrowd the farm market bins, piled deep and high. When it's too hot to fuss in the kitchen and I want dinner on the table quickly, I rely on the tomato harvest to make Spaghetti alla Checca (page 168). The tomatoes are blanched for mere seconds, just long enough to peel away their skins without compromising their ripe flesh. Paired with fresh basil from the yard and quality mozzarella, it is a dish that makes everyone happy.

If you happen to find yourself with over-ripened tomatoes, keep them—and don't bypass them at the market either. There's a no-cook Italian sauce for precisely these super-juicy tomatoes. As my grandmother would often say, "waste not, want not." When grated raw and perfumed with fresh garlic and a robust extra-virgin olive oil, you will have a new favorite pasta dish, Pasta with Raw Sauce and Ricotta Salata (page 172).

When the mood strikes me to whip up a fresh summer pasta dough, I opt for a little squid ink for a luxurious midnight-colored pasta, subtly flavored with the brine of the sea. It pairs beautifully with seafood when we want to hold onto our days at the sea a little longer. Be sure to try my Fresh Squid Ink Pasta with Clams, Garlic and Summer Tomatoes (page 176).

Blueberry and Raw Sweet Corn Orzo with Basil and Thyme

Have you ever taken a bite of raw sweet corn fresh from the stalk? Quality farm-fresh corn is succulently sweet as-is—there's no need for butter or roasting. In this side dish, I use raw local sweet corn that's been trimmed from the cob and tossed together with fresh summer herbs, hand-picked blueberries and seasonal leafy greens. Consider adding torn pieces of fresh mozzarella and serve it alongside your BBQ favorites.

Serves 4–6

2 tbsp (30 ml) fresh lemon juice

¼ cup (60 ml) plus 1 tbsp (15 ml) extra-virgin olive oil, divided, plus more as needed

½ cup (10 g) fresh basil leaves, roughly chopped

2 sprigs fresh thyme leaves, roughly chopped

Kosher salt and freshly ground pepper, to taste

1 lb (454 g) dried orzo

6 oz (170 g) fresh blueberries

3 ears sweet corn, husked and kernels cut from the cob

Leafy greens of choice (kale, Swiss chard, etc.), desired amount

In a small bowl, make the vinaigrette by combining the lemon juice, olive oil, basil, thyme, salt and pepper. Whisk well to combine and emulsify. Taste and adjust the seasonings.

Bring a large pot of water to a boil. Generously salt the water, add the orzo and cook until al dente, tender yet firm to the bite, according to the package directions. Drain and briefly rinse the orzo with cold water to stop the cooking and to remove some of the starch. Drain well again.

Add the cooled orzo to a large serving bowl, drizzle lightly with 1 tablespoon (15 ml) of the olive oil to prevent sticking and toss well.

Add the blueberries, raw sweet corn kernels and the fresh greens, and briefly toss to combine. Drizzle in the vinaigrette and toss gently to coat. Serve immediately, drizzling with more olive oil if necessary to help loosen the orzo.

Penne Lisce with Blackberries, Balsamic and Basil

Here is another recipe to highlight the berry harvest of summer and the delightful, yet unexpected, combination of delicate fruit and pasta. Again, pasta is used as a supporting ingredient, providing a substantial base for the sweet burst of blackberries and tender, peppery greens. The contrast of balsamic vinegar and red onion help to balance the flavor profile in this dish.

Serves 4–6

¼ cup (60 ml) extra-virgin olive oil, plus more as needed

2–3 tbsp (30–45 ml) balsamic vinegar

Kosher salt and freshly ground pepper, to taste

12 oz (340 g) dry penne lisce (or any other short pasta)

4 cups (80 g) packed arugula

Handful of fresh basil, roughly chopped

1 small red onion, slivered

Fresh mozzarella, torn (desired amount)

1½ cups (216 g) fresh blackberries

In a small bowl, prepare the vinaigrette by combining the olive oil, balsamic vinegar, salt and pepper, and whisk well until emulsified, less than a minute. Set aside.

Bring a large pot of water to a boil. Generously salt the water and add the pasta. Cook until al dente, tender yet firm to the bite, according to the package directions. Drain and lightly rinse under cool water. Drain again. Transfer the pasta to a large serving bowl.

Add the arugula, basil, onion and the desired amount of torn mozzarella to the pasta. Gently drizzle with the vinaigrette and toss together. To serve, divide into individual bowls and garnish with blackberries. Drizzle the top with more olive oil if desired.

Cook's Notes: *Consider using white balsamic vinegar if you don't want to stain the pasta with dark vinegar.*

Sweet Plums, Cucumber and Blue Cheese Pasta Salad

Plump and heavy plums, deeply purple like the shadows of a summer evening, begin to fill the bins at my local farm market in midsummer. With plums in hand, I grab a farm-fresh cucumber and snip some basil and thyme from outside of my kitchen door. A medium pasta, like strozzapreti, an elongated cavatelli, is perfect for keeping uniform shape with the other ingredients, making it easier to load up your fork. Its twisty, scroll-like shape holds to the fragrant olive oil and vinegar, and the creamy blue cheese adds a complementary bite, bringing this light summer dish all together.

Serves 4–6

Kosher salt, to taste

1 lb (454 g) strozzapreti (or other medium pasta shape)

¼ cup (60 ml) extra-virgin olive oil, plus more for drizzling

1 cucumber, peeled, halved lengthwise and thinly sliced

1 small red onion, thinly sliced

10–15 basil leaves, roughly chopped

10–15 mint leaves, finely chopped

3 tbsp (45 ml) white wine vinegar

Freshly ground pepper, to taste

3 whole ripe plums, pitted and sliced into thin wedges

Blue cheese, desired amount crumbled, to garnish

Bring a large pot of water to a boil. Generously salt the water and add the pasta. Cook until al dente, tender yet firm to the bite, according to the package directions. Drain and briefly rinse the pasta under cool running water to remove excess starch and to stop the cooking. Drain again and add the pasta to a large serving bowl.

Add the olive oil to the pasta and gently mix to incorporate, adding more oil if needed. Add the cucumber, red onion, basil, mint, vinegar, salt and pepper, and toss to combine. Taste and adjust the seasonings. Top with the sliced plums.

Serve with desired amount of blue cheese garnish, passing the rest at the table, and top with an extra drizzle of olive oil.

Cook's Notes: *Adding the plums last or using them to top each serving will help keep the plums intact. If the plums are soft and ripe, adding them too early on and tossing may compromise them, making them fall apart, and they'll impart a pinkish hue to the pasta.*

Mezze Penne with Grilled Peaches and Rosemary

Summer peaches are grilled to perfection and added to bacon, quality mozzarella and vibrant summer greens in this sweet and savory late-summer dish. Mezze penne, a shorter version of traditional penne, makes it easy to pick up a little bit of everything in this dish, though traditional penne would work well too. A seasonal dressing infused with local honey and fresh rosemary is the aromatic finishing touch on this easy-to-prepare summer dish that pairs beautifully with grilled chicken.

Serves 4–6

¼ cup (60 ml) plus 2 tbsp (30 ml) extra-virgin olive oil, plus more as needed

3 tbsp (45 ml) freshly squeezed lemon juice

2 tbsp (30 ml) honey

1 large clove garlic, finely grated

2–3 small sprigs fresh rosemary, stems discarded and leaves finely chopped

Kosher salt and freshly ground pepper, to taste

12 oz (340 g) mezze penne

8 oz (227 g) nitrate-free sliced bacon

3 firm peaches, halved, pitted and sliced into wedges

1 shallot, thinly sliced

2 cups (60 g) arugula, washed and dried

2 cups (60 g) packed baby spinach, washed and dried

Fresh mozzarella, roughly torn

In a medium bowl, add ¼ cup (60 ml) of olive oil and the lemon juice and whisk well. Drizzle in the honey, garlic and chopped rosemary and season to taste with salt and pepper; whisk well until emulsified. Set aside.

Bring a large pot of water to a boil. Generously salt the water and add the pasta. Cook until al dente, tender yet firm to the bite, according to the package directions. Drain and briefly rinse under cool water to stop the cooking and remove some of the starch. Drain well again. Transfer the pasta to a large serving bowl. Drizzle with 2 tablespoons (30 ml) of olive oil, toss to coat and set aside.

In the meantime, prepare the bacon as per the package directions to desired doneness. Transfer the cooked bacon onto a paper towel–lined plate to cool. Break into 1- to 2-inch (2.5- to 5-cm) pieces and set aside.

To grill the peaches, lightly brush the cut sides with olive oil and set on an outdoor grill over a medium flame, or on a stove-top grill pan, until grill marks appear, about 3 minutes each side. Add the peaches to the serving bowl with the pasta.

Add the shallot, bacon, arugula, spinach and mozzarella to the serving bowl with the pasta and peaches. Gently toss to mix. Drizzle with the dressing and gently toss again. Serve with more olive oil, if desired.

Pasta with Sausage and Broccolini in Roasted Red Pepper Sauce

The flavors of summer vary wildly from the sweet to the savory. In this dish, I've combined the sweet succulence of sun-dried tomatoes with perfectly charred roasted red peppers. Pasta water, as usual, is the liquid gold that will emulsify the sauce, giving you control of the consistency and bringing it all together. The best part of this recipe, though, is the garnish of goat cheese and how it melts slow and creamy as it mingles with the warm pasta that rests beneath. All of this comes together in the time it takes to boil the pasta—it is summer ease at its most flavorful.

Serves 4–6

12 oz (340 g) thinly sliced roasted red peppers (homemade or jarred)

7 oz (198 g) sun-dried tomatoes

¼ tsp red pepper flakes

1 clove garlic, smashed

¼ tsp kosher salt, plus more to taste

¼ cup (60 ml) plus 1 tbsp (15 ml) extra-virgin olive oil, divided, plus more for drizzling

1 lb (454 g) ziti rigate (or other short pasta of choice)

¾ lb (340 g) sweet Italian sausage, casings removed

1 cup (240 ml) vegetable broth

½ lb (225 g) broccolini, rinsed, bottom third of the stems removed, thick stems cut in half lengthwise

Freshly ground pepper, to taste

Grated local cheese with a hard and sharp profile or Parmigiano-Reggiano, to garnish

In a food processor, pulse together the roasted red peppers, sun-dried tomatoes, red pepper flakes, garlic and salt. With the food processor running, slowly drizzle in the ¼ cup (60 ml) of olive oil. Set aside.

Bring a large pot of water to a boil. Generously salt the water and add the pasta. Cook until just shy of al dente, tender yet firm to the bite, according to the package directions. Reserve 1 cup (240 ml) of the pasta water before draining. Drain well.

In the meantime, in a large skillet, heat 1 tablespoon (15 ml) of olive oil over medium-high heat. Using a wooden spoon, crumble the sausage into the skillet and cook, breaking it up into bite-sized pieces, until lightly browned and almost fully cooked, about 7 minutes.

Reduce the heat to medium and add the vegetable broth and broccolini, then bring to a boil. Scrape the bottom of the pan to deglaze any flavorful brown bits that may have accumulated. Cover and cook, stirring halfway through the cooking time, until the broccolini is tender but still crisp, 5 to 6 minutes. Season with salt and freshly ground pepper.

Add the sun-dried tomato and roasted red pepper mixture to the skillet. Stir well to combine. Add the pasta and ½ cup (120 ml) of the reserved pasta water and gently fold and toss together to coat well. Add the rest of the reserved pasta water if needed and toss together again, until most of the liquid is absorbed, 1 minute. The consistency should be loose, not pasty.

To serve, top with the grated cheese and a generous drizzle of olive oil.

Rigatoni with Rosemary-Roasted Eggplant and Blackened Cherries

Eggplant is a wonderful meatless option. It adds substance and texture, and I often rely on this dish when eggplant is in season. Branches of fresh-snipped rosemary add a layer of earthy flavor and sweet summer cherries are intensified when their delicate skin is caramelized. The tubular shape of rigatoni is the perfect vessel for all these wonderful ingredients to tuck into, picking up lots of flavor with each forkful. A creamy blue cheese neutralizes the sweetness and completes the dish.

Serves 4–6

1 large eggplant, peeled and cubed into 1-inch (2.5-cm) pieces

Kosher salt, as needed

¼ cup (60 ml) plus 2–3 tbsp (30–45 ml) extra-virgin olive oil, divided

Freshly ground pepper, to taste

½ tsp fresh rosemary, finely chopped

15–20 Bing cherries, pitted

1 lb (454 g) rigatoni

1 tbsp (15 g) butter

1 small onion, halved and thinly sliced

1 small clove garlic, finely grated

Blue cheese, crumbled, to garnish

Handful of fresh lemon basil, slivered, to garnish

Place the eggplant in a colander and generously sprinkle with salt. Salting will remove the bitterness that is natural in a larger eggplant. Smaller eggplants, with less or no seeds, will not need to be salted. With clean hands, give a gentle toss and leave the eggplant to sit at room temperature for 30 minutes. Once moisture begins to bead on the eggplant, rinse well and pat dry, removing as much excess water as possible.

Preheat the oven to 425°F (220°C).

Arrange the eggplant pieces on a baking sheet lined with parchment paper or a silicone mat and drizzle 1 to 2 tablespoons (15 to 30 ml) of olive oil to massage evenly onto the eggplant. Sprinkle with salt, pepper and rosemary, and toss to coat.

On a second baking sheet lined with parchment paper or a silicone mat, spread the cherries and drizzle with 1 tablespoon (15 ml) of olive oil to massage evenly onto the cherries.

Place the baking sheets in the oven and roast for 15 minutes. Remove the cherries from the oven and set aside to cool. Gently toss the eggplant and return to the oven for another 10 to 15 minutes. The eggplant should be crisp in some areas, golden and caramelized in others. Remove from the oven and set aside.

Meanwhile, bring a large pot of water to a boil. Generously salt the water and add the pasta. Cook until just shy of al dente, tender yet firm to the bite, according to the package directions. Reserve ½ cup (120 ml) of the pasta water before draining. Drain well.

In a large 12-inch (30-cm) skillet with deep sides, heat ¼ cup (60 ml) of olive oil and the butter over low-medium heat until the oil is hot and shimmery and the butter is melted. Add the onion and season with salt, then sauté until tender and beginning to caramelize, about 10 minutes. Add the garlic and cook until fragrant, 30 seconds. Add the pasta and ¼ cup (60 ml) of pasta water to the skillet, tossing to combine. Add more of the reserved water only to help loosen the pasta, if necessary. Add a few turns of freshly ground pepper and gently toss again.

Transfer the eggplant to the pasta, giving another gentle toss to combine. To serve, garnish with the desired amount of both blue cheese and roasted cherries. Top with slivers of fresh lemon basil.

Tuna Pasta with Tomatoes and Basil

Sometimes it's the simplest of recipes that are the best. That certainly applies to this recipe. Since most, if not all, of the ingredients listed are kitchen staples, tuna pasta is a quick go-to meal in my house when we need a fast but substantial lunch or for when a guest unexpectedly stops by. This is a very forgiving recipe and can be adjusted to suit your preferences. It is best when served chilled or at room temperature. Enjoy as is or over a bed of leafy greens lightly dressed in olive oil.

Serves 6

Kosher salt

1 lb (454 g) fusilli pasta

2 tbsp (30 ml) extra-virgin olive oil, plus more if needed

2 (5-oz [142-g]) cans white albacore tuna, packed in olive oil

⅓ cup (77 g) mayonnaise, plus more if needed

2 tbsp (30 ml) white wine vinegar, or more as desired

Freshly ground pepper

1 pint (295 g) ripe cherry or grape tomatoes, halved

½ red onion, thinly sliced

2 tbsp (20 g) capers, rinsed

⅓ cup (60 g) Sicilian olives, pitted and halved, plus 1 tbsp (15 ml) of olive brine (if using jarred)

Handful of fresh basil (about 10 leaves), roughly chopped

Bring a large pot of water to a boil. Generously salt the water and add the pasta. Cook until al dente, tender yet firm to the bite, according to the package directions. Drain. Rinse under cool water and drain well again.

Transfer the pasta to a large serving bowl and add the olive oil, stir to incorporate and set aside.

To a separate medium bowl, add the tuna, breaking it up with a fork into desired-size pieces. If packed in quality olive oil, add the flavorful oil as well; there's no need to drain.

Add the mayonnaise and vinegar to the tuna and mix well to incorporate. Lightly season with salt and pepper. It will look a bit wet at this point until mixed with the pasta. Add the tuna to the pasta. Toss to combine.

To the tuna pasta, add the tomatoes, red onion, capers, olives, olive brine and basil; toss well to combine. Taste and adjust the seasonings, if necessary, keeping in mind that the olives and capers are already salty in taste. Add more mayo if needed. Add more olive oil if necessary to loosen the pasta. The pasta should be creamy, but not too thick.

Cortecce with Seared Swordfish and Summer Herbs

On those hot summer days when the afternoons are long and it's too hot to fuss in the kitchen, yet I still want to create something extra special, I rely on this recipe. Swordfish and pasta go together like the salty sea air and the shores of Sicily. I toss in capers for their desired brine and plump cherry tomatoes that burst warm with every bite. In the true ease of summer, this is ready to be served by the time the pasta is al dente. If you can get your hands on heirloom tomatoes, their varying hues will add color and interest to this dish.

Serves 4–6

Kosher salt

1 lb (454 g) cortecce (or any medium-cut pasta)

¼ cup (60 ml) extra-virgin olive oil, plus more for drizzling

¼ tsp red pepper flakes

2 cloves garlic, smashed

1 lb (454 g) swordfish steak, about 1 inch (2.5 cm) thick

Freshly ground black pepper, to taste

¼ cup (60 ml) Sauvignon Blanc

½ lb (225 g) cherry or grape tomatoes, halved

1 cup (180 g) large black olives, halved

2 tbsp (20 g) capers, rinsed

Handful of fresh parsley, roughly chopped

Handful of fresh basil, roughly chopped

2 sprigs fresh thyme, stems removed

Bring a large pot of water to a boil. Generously salt the water and add the pasta. Cook until just shy of al dente, tender yet firm to the bite, according to the package directions. Reserve 1 cup (240 ml) of the pasta water before draining. Drain well.

In the meantime, over low–medium heat, add the olive oil to a large 12-inch (30-cm) skillet with deep sides. When the oil is hot and shimmery, add the red pepper flakes and garlic and sauté until the garlic turns golden, being careful not to let it burn as the flavor will be bitter, about 5 minutes. Remove the garlic and discard.

Season both sides of the swordfish with salt and pepper. Add the swordfish to the skillet to brown evenly, 4 to 5 minutes per side. Using a fork, roughly flake the swordfish, leaving it in large bite-sized pieces. Discard the skin.

Remove the skillet from the heat to add the wine, then return to a medium heat and gently deglaze the pan by scraping up any brown bits that may have accumulated. Add the tomatoes, olives and capers and simmer until the tomatoes soften and warm through, about 3 minutes. Turn off the heat. Add the parsley, basil and thyme, then toss to combine.

Add the pasta to the skillet along with ¼ cup (60 ml) of the reserved pasta water. Toss together gently. Use more of the reserved pasta water to loosen the pasta, if necessary. Taste and adjust the seasonings. To serve, drizzle generously with olive oil.

Gemelli with Roasted Garlic Scapes and Caramelized Tomatoes

Oh, those elusive garlic scapes! These green curlicues are in season in early summer, and their time with us is fleeting. If you aren't familiar with garlic scapes, they are the flower stalk that grows out from the head of garlic. They're slender with hues of light and darker green, a whimsical twisty stem and a slender and narrowing bud. They are milder in flavor than garlic but can still be used in the same way. I prefer to keep their shape mostly intact, opting not to puree them as so many recipes seem to do. Their unique shape makes them memorable and adds a flair to a very simple pasta dish.

Serves 4–6

Kosher salt, to taste

1 lb (454 g) gemelli (or any other medium pasta)

4 tbsp (60 ml) extra-virgin olive oil, divided, plus more for drizzling

10 garlic scapes, ends trimmed (including any straggly parts on the bud)

1 pint (295 g) grape tomatoes, halved

Freshly ground black pepper, to taste

Handful of basil (or desired amount), roughly chopped

Juice of 1 lemon

Grated Parmigiano-Reggiano or local cheese with a hard and sharp profile, to garnish

Preheat the oven to 425°F (220°C).

Bring a large pot of water to a boil. Generously salt the water and add the pasta. Cook until just shy of al dente, tender yet firm to the bite, according to the package directions. Reserve ½ cup (120 ml) of the pasta water before draining. Drain well. Drizzle the pasta with 2 tablespoons (30 ml) of olive oil to prevent sticking and set aside.

In the meantime, prepare a baking sheet lined with parchment paper or a silicone mat and add the garlic scapes and tomatoes. Drizzle with 2 tablespoons (30 ml) of olive oil and massage onto the garlic scapes evenly. Season with salt and pepper. Roast for 20 minutes or until the garlic scapes have started to crisp and the tomatoes begin to burst and blister. Remove from the oven and give the garlic scapes a few minutes to cool to the touch. Using a sharp knife, cut them into sizes comparable to the pasta (it will make picking up a forkful much easier), being mindful to leave the curlicue shapes intact as much as possible—purely for aesthetic reasons.

Toss the garlic scapes and the tomatoes together with the pasta. Add ¼ cup (60 ml) of the reserved pasta water, basil and lemon juice, then toss together again to incorporate. Only add more of the reserved pasta water to loosen the pasta if necessary.

Serve with a generous drizzle of olive oil and grated cheese.

Tagliatelle and Shaved Zucchini in Lavender-Thyme Cream

One might not consider lavender a seasonal ingredient. I'd certainly beg to differ. I wait with bated breath for the summer announcement from Monica at Orchard View Lavender Farm that the lavender is ready for harvesting. If you think of lavender as an herb, and not just an aromatic flower, you'll find many uses for it. A little goes a long way to add a light floral undertone, and when paired with thyme, the flavors are perfectly balanced. Lavender should only ever accent the flavors of the dish and not compete with them. Tagliatelle is my pasta of choice for this dish as it blends and twists beautifully with the ribbons of zucchini. Enjoy this dish as-is or alongside a summer salad and crispy herbed chicken.

Serves 4

1 large zucchini, halved lengthwise and peeled

Kosher salt, to taste

12 oz (340 g) tagliatelle (pappardelle would work too)

¼ cup (60 ml) extra-virgin olive oil, plus more for drizzling

1 medium shallot, thinly sliced

Freshly ground pepper, to taste

1 heaping tsp roughly chopped fresh culinary lavender flowers

1 heaping tsp roughly chopped fresh thyme leaves

½ cup (120 ml) Sauvignon Blanc

½ cup (120 ml) chicken broth

2 tbsp (30 ml) light cream

2 tbsp (30 g) butter

Grated Parmigiano-Reggiano or local cheese with a hard and sharp profile, to garnish

First prepare the zucchini. Use a vegetable peeler or kitchen mandolin to thinly shave the zucchini lengthwise. When it becomes too thin to continue to shave, finely chop what remains. Set the chopped pieces aside and divide the shavings.

Bring a large pot of water to a boil. Generously salt the water and add the pasta. Cook until just shy of al dente, tender yet firm to the bite, according to the package directions. Reserve ½ cup (120 ml) of the pasta water before draining. Drain well.

Meanwhile, in a large 12-inch (30-cm) skillet over low-medium heat, warm the olive oil until it is hot and shimmery, then add the shallot and half of the shaved zucchini and any chopped pieces. Season with salt and a few turns of freshly ground pepper and gently toss to combine. Cook, stirring often, until the shallot begins to caramelize and the zucchini is softened, about 10 minutes. Add the lavender and thyme, stirring again to mix, about 1 minute, to incorporate the flavors and to lightly toast the herbs.

Remove the skillet from the heat to add the wine. Return to moderate heat, cooking until the wine reduces by half, 5 minutes. The zucchini will greatly soften and break down, thickening up the oil and creating a base for the sauce. Add the broth and the remaining zucchini shavings and bring to a low simmer, cooking to heat through, 2 to 3 minutes.

Add the pasta and ¼ cup (60 ml) of the reserved pasta water to the skillet and toss well. Add the light cream and butter. Toss well to combine and to finish cooking the pasta, about 1 minute. Only use more of the reserved water to loosen the pasta if necessary. The texture should be silky and lightly creamy with movement. The pasta will continue to thicken upon standing.

Top each serving with freshly grated cheese.

Cook's Notes: *Not all lavender is created equal! Be sure to choose culinary grade, organic lavender for cooking.*

Pasta with Caramelized Squash and Zucchini Blossoms

When tender zucchini and yellow squash are cooked down and caramelized, they all but melt, becoming a savory and velvety sauce, perfect to coat long strands of pasta. As for the blossoms, if you're lucky enough to grow zucchini yourself, you can harvest these blossoms from your own backyard. Otherwise, you're likely to find them at a farmers' market. When the blossoms are salted and lightly cooked, they make a beautiful addition.

Serves 4

10–15 zucchini blossoms

2 tbsp (30 g) butter

Kosher salt, as needed

12 oz (340 g) bucatini (or any long pasta)

¼ cup (60 ml) extra-virgin olive oil

3 medium cloves garlic, smashed

2 large shallots, thinly sliced

1 zucchini, ends trimmed, quartered lengthwise and thinly sliced

1 yellow squash, ends trimmed, quartered lengthwise and thinly sliced

Freshly ground pepper

1 cup (240 ml) vegetable broth

Grated ricotta salata (or pecorino), to garnish

Handful of basil (about 10 leaves), roughly torn, to garnish

Gently remove the hard pistil from within each zucchini flower and cut away the stem. Since we are not stuffing the blossoms, if you find opening the petals difficult to remove the pistil, simply cut the blossom in half lengthwise and remove it. Very gently rinse the delicate blossoms under cool running water, carefully shake the excess water from the inside of the blossoms and let them dry on paper towels.

Heat the butter in a large 12-inch (30-cm) skillet over moderate heat. When the butter is hot and beginning to foam, add the zucchini blossoms in a single layer and briefly cook until wilted, about 30 seconds. Use a slotted spoon or tongs to transfer the blossoms to paper towels and set aside. Lightly season with salt. Set the skillet aside, along with any butter left in the pan—you'll use it again for the onions and zucchini.

In the meantime, bring a large pot of water to a boil. Generously salt the water and add the pasta. Cook until just shy of al dente, tender yet firm to the bite, according to the package directions. Reserve ½ cup (120 ml) of the pasta water before draining. Drain well.

In the same buttered skillet used for the blossoms, warm the olive oil over low-medium heat. When the oil is hot and shimmery, add the smashed garlic, shallots, zucchini and yellow squash. Season to taste with salt and a few good turns of ground pepper and briefly stir. Let the vegetables sit undisturbed until they have begun to sear, about 6 minutes. Gently stir again and continue to cook, stirring only occasionally, until the vegetables are golden brown and caramelized, about 25 minutes. The garlic will be very soft at this point; use the back of your cooking spoon to mash the garlic into bits, and stir to combine. While some of the vegetables will have crisped, many will begin to fall apart and possibly even stick to the pan a little—that's the "pulp" that will come together in the hot broth and the reserved pasta water to make a flavorful and silky sauce for the pasta.

Add the vegetable broth to the pan and bring it to a boil, then turn off the heat. Add the pasta to the skillet along with ¼ cup (60 ml) of the reserved pasta water and toss to coat well. Use the remaining pasta water to loosen the pasta, if necessary. Taste and adjust the seasonings.

Divide into individual plates or bowls and top each serving with zucchini blossoms and a generous grating of ricotta salata and basil.

Fettuccine with Fresh Corn, Blistered Tomatoes and Thyme

This dish relies on good-quality sweet summer corn. The flavors in this dish are bright and warm like the sunny fields in which the corn grows. We'll use cherry tomatoes and a splash of white wine for good measure. This is a perfect light summer lunch or dinner.

Serves 4–6

¼ cup (60 ml) extra-virgin olive oil, plus more for drizzling

1 pint (295 g) fresh grape or cherry tomatoes

Kosher salt

2 large shallots, thinly sliced

½ cup (120 ml) Sauvignon Blanc

2 tbsp (30 g) Dijon mustard

½ cup (120 ml) chicken broth, plus more as needed

3 cups (450 g) corn kernels (from about 4 large ears of corn, divided)

Freshly ground black pepper

1 lb (454 g) fettuccine (or other long pasta)

3 tbsp (45 g) butter

1 tsp chopped fresh thyme, plus extra sprigs to garnish

In a large 12-inch (30-cm) heavy-bottomed skillet over low–medium heat, warm the olive oil until it is hot and shimmery. Carefully add the tomatoes and lightly season with salt. Leave the tomatoes undisturbed for 1 minute, lightly stir and then leave them alone again for 1 minute more. The tomatoes should be slightly charred and blistered. Use a slotted spoon to remove the tomatoes from the skillet and set aside.

To the same pan, add the shallots and cook, stirring often, until tender and caramelized, 10 minutes. Remove the skillet from the heat to add the wine. Scrape the bottom of the pan to deglaze any flavorful brown bits that may have accumulated. Add the Dijon, ½ cup (120 ml) of the broth and all but ½ cup (88 g) of the corn kernels. Cook until the corn is warmed through, about 2 minutes. Season to taste with salt and pepper. Allow the mixture to cool somewhat before adding to a high-powered blender. Keep the skillet on hand for later use. Half fill the blender's canister and puree the mixture until smooth, working in batches if necessary. The puree should be thick but loose enough to still pour with ease. If too thick, thin with more broth. Set aside.

In the meantime, bring a large pot of water to a boil. Generously salt the water and add the pasta. Cook until just shy of al dente, tender yet firm to the bite, according to the package directions. Reserve 1 cup (240 ml) of the pasta water before draining. Drain well.

In the skillet you used earlier, warm the butter over medium heat. Cook until melted. Add the remaining corn kernels and the corn puree and cook, gently stirring, to warm the contents through, about 3 minutes. Add the cooked pasta to the skillet along with the reserved pasta water. Toss gently until the pasta absorbs most of the liquid and has finished cooking, about 1 minute. The pasta will continue to thicken upon standing.

Add the chopped thyme and gently toss to combine. Add the tomatoes back to the pan and toss again; the warmth from the pasta will warm the tomatoes through. To serve, garnish with fresh thyme sprigs (optional).

Cook's Notes: *Adding grilled corn that has been slightly charred adds another level of flavor!*

Cucumber Pasta Salad with Creamy Dill

This pasta salad is a wonderfully simple addition to your summer fare. Crisp cucumbers, sour cream and mayonnaise are enhanced with fresh-cut dill and a squeeze of bright lemon to add a refreshingly fragrant element to this easy, full-flavored and creamy side dish. I chose gemelli for its twisted shape and for how the dressing sneaks into the folds as I sweep the pasta across my plate to scoop-up all that delectable flavor.

Serves 4–6

1 cucumber

½ cup (115 g) sour cream

½ cup (115 g) mayonnaise

2 tbsp (30 ml) fresh squeezed lemon juice

1 medium shallot, thinly sliced

2 tbsp (6 g) roughly chopped fresh dill

½ tsp kosher salt, plus more for cooking pasta

Freshly ground pepper, to taste

12 oz (340 g) gemelli (or other medium-cut pasta)

Peel the cucumber and halve it lengthwise. Use a small spoon to scoop out the seeds and discard. Slice crosswise in ¼-inch (6-mm) pieces and set aside.

In a large bowl, combine the sour cream, mayonnaise, lemon juice, shallot and fresh dill. Stir well to mix. Add the cucumber slices. Season with salt and pepper. Mix together again. Set aside.

In the meantime, bring a large pot of water to a boil. Generously salt the water and add the pasta. Cook until al dente, tender yet firm to the bite, according to the package directions. Drain the pasta and rinse under cool water to remove the starches and to stop the cooking.

Add the pasta to the large bowl with the cucumber dressing. Taste and adjust the seasonings, if necessary. The texture should be light and creamy. Serve at room temperature.

Spaghetti alla Checca

Here is another favorite recipe to honor tomatoes in all their raw summery goodness. Checca simply refers to the use of uncooked tomatoes with fresh herbs and pasta. A proper checca sauce is always made with quality mozzarella and perfectly ripe backyard or farm-market tomatoes, not the tight and watery kind. I prefer to just barely scald the tomatoes to easily remove their skins, without compromising their integrity. I recall this dish from my childhood and each twisted and tangled forkful tastes like home to me.

Serves 4–6

2 lbs (907 g) ripe tomatoes (about 4 medium tomatoes)

1 clove garlic, finely grated

Handful of fresh basil leaves (about 10), roughly chopped

4 sprigs fresh thyme, center stems removed and leaves finely chopped

4 sprigs fresh oregano, center stems removed and leaves finely chopped

¼ cup (60 ml) plus 2 tbsp (30 ml) extra-virgin olive oil, divided, plus more as needed

Kosher salt and freshly ground pepper, to taste

1 lb (454 g) spaghetti (or use any long pasta of choice)

8 oz (227 g) mozzarella, roughly torn into bite-sized pieces

Fill a large pot halfway with water and bring to a boil. Use a sharp paring knife to slice through the skin at the bottom of each tomato, making an "x." When the water comes to a boil, turn off the heat and add the tomatoes to the pot for about 30 seconds—this is just long enough to soften the skins, making them easy to peel, without compromising their flesh. It's helpful to use a medium-sized mesh sieve to lower the tomatoes into the pot and again to scoop them back out.

Carefully remove the tomatoes from the water and set aside. Once the tomatoes are cool to the touch, peel, core and seed them. Reserve all their liquid by adding the pulpy seeds that have been removed to a mesh sieve, pressing to release any of their juice, then discard the seeds. Chop the tomatoes, leaving them large enough to remain the star of the recipe, though sized to easily enjoy.

Add the tomatoes and juices to a large bowl. Add the garlic, herbs, ¼ cup (60 ml) of olive oil, a generous pinch of salt and a few turns of freshly ground pepper. Toss to combine. Cover and let the mixture sit at least 30 minutes at room temperature for the flavors to combine; the longer it sits the more the flavors will develop.

In the meantime, bring a large pot of water to a boil. Generously salt the water and add the pasta. Cook until al dente, tender yet firm to the bite, according to the package directions. Reserve ¼ cup (60 ml) of the pasta water before draining. Drain well.

Add the pasta to a large serving bowl and generously drizzle with roughly 2 tablespoons (30 ml) of olive oil. Add the tomato mixture, tossing gently to combine. Add the reserved pasta water, tossing together once more. Use more olive oil to loosen the pasta, if necessary—this will vary depending upon the juiciness of the tomatoes used.

Add the mozzarella and briefly toss to combine. Allow a minute or two for the warmth of the pasta to barely melt the cheese.

Serve immediately, drizzling each serving lightly with more olive oil, if desired. The pasta will continue to absorb the liquid as it sits, so be sure to toss it every now and again, scooping up from the bottom.

Tortellini Summer Salad with Basil Vinaigrette

Every summer I grow several varieties of basil in terra cotta pots. Once the heat of July takes over, my basil grows wild and needs to be harvested almost daily. When I have too much, which is often, I lean on this vinaigrette. In keeping with the ease of summer, I've paired it with a simple but filling cheese tortellini and a few other simple seasonal ingredients. Enjoy as-is or pair with your favorite summer main course.

Serves 4—6

5 oz (142 g) leafy greens (any type, mixed), rinsed and roughly chopped if leaves are large

½ lb (225 g) cherry or grape tomatoes, halved or quartered

3 tbsp (34 g) grated pecorino cheese

2 cups (48 g) packed basil, stems removed

2 tbsp (30 ml) lemon juice, freshly squeezed

½ cup (120 ml) extra-virgin olive oil

1 shallot, halved

½ tsp kosher salt, plus more as needed

Freshly ground pepper, to taste

12 oz (340 g) cheese tortellini

Fresh mozzarella, roughly torn

Add the greens to a large serving bowl—one that is large enough to later accommodate the tortellini too. Add the tomatoes and grated cheese and toss to combine. Set aside.

To make the vinaigrette, add the basil, lemon juice, olive oil, shallot, ½ teaspoon salt and several turns of freshly ground pepper to a high-speed blender or food processor and pulse until well combined. Taste and adjust the seasonings, if necessary.

Bring a large pot of water to a boil. Generously salt, then add the tortellini. Cook according to the package directions. Drain, giving the tortellini a brief rinse to stop the cooking and to remove some of the starch.

Add the tortellini to the serving bowl with the greens. Drizzle enough of the vinaigrette over the tortellini to coat well and toss to combine, passing the rest of the vinaigrette at the table. Add the torn mozzarella, give another toss and serve.

Pasta with Raw Sauce and Ricotta Salata

The tomatoes of late summer are often heavy and plump, and many have over-ripened, perhaps with tender and bruised flesh. These are often the tomatoes passed over for a firmer, more desired choice. However, it's these over-ripened tomatoes that have the most to offer this dish. When heavily ripened tomatoes are grated raw, infused with garlic, seasoned with salt and fresh cracked pepper, drizzled with a full-bodied extra-virgin olive oil and warmed only by the tossing of the pasta, you'll have the taste of a slow Italian summer in your own backyard.

Serves 4–6

3 lbs (1.4 kg) very ripe tomatoes

½ cup (120 ml) extra-virgin olive oil

1 clove garlic, finely grated

1 tbsp (15 ml) balsamic vinegar

Handful of basil leaves (roughly 10), slivered, plus more to garnish

1 tsp kosher salt, plus more as needed

½ tsp freshly ground black pepper

1 lb (454 g) thin linguine (or any pasta of choice)

Grated ricotta salata (substitute with pecorino), to garnish

With a sharp knife, thinly slice off the bottom round of each tomato. Over a medium bowl, start with the cut side of the tomato and grate it against the large holes on a box grater. Grate the tomato down to the skin and stem, then discard.

Add the olive oil, garlic, vinegar and basil to the bowl with the grated tomatoes, season with 1 teaspoon of salt and ½ teaspoon freshly ground pepper and stir well. Cover and let the mixture sit so the flavors can come together, at least 30 minutes at room temperature or refrigerated overnight. If opting for overnight, let the mixture come to room temperature before using.

Bring a large pot of water to a boil. Generously salt the water and add the pasta. Cook until al dente, tender yet firm to the bite, according to the package directions. Reserve ¼ cup (60 ml) of the pasta water before draining. Drain well.

Transfer the pasta to a large serving bowl and add the raw tomato mixture to the hot pasta, tossing well to combine and coat the pasta. Add half of the reserved pasta water and toss again to combine. Only use the remaining pasta water to loosen the pasta if necessary.

To serve, top with basil and a generous grating of ricotta salata or pecorino. The pasta will continue to absorb a bit upon standing.

Cook's Notes: *Consider coring and chopping more tomatoes as a garnish, adding some meatier pieces to this raw sauce.*

Fresh Beetroot Pasta with Lemon Basil and Beet Greens

Red beets impart a mild earthiness to fresh pasta; the flavor is perfectly subtle but the real reason to make this fresh pasta is the impressive color! The jewel-toned crimson tendrils of fettuccine make for an outstanding table presentation and elevate an otherwise very simple dish. This dough can be used for ravioli, spaghetti or whatever type of pasta you desire. When storing beets, you need to remove their stems and leafy greens, as they pull moisture away from the beet. These greens are typically discarded. However, they are perfectly edible! In fact, they look and taste a lot like Swiss chard. When buying or harvesting beets, you'll want a bunch with sturdy, crisp leaves that are well intact. Sauté them like you would any other leafy green.

Serves 4–6

Beet greens, from the bunch

2 beets, from a bunch

Basic Pasta Dough (page 16)

Cider vinegar, to taste

Kosher salt and freshly ground pepper, to taste

¼ cup (60 ml) extra-virgin olive oil, plus more as needed

¼ tsp red pepper flakes

1 clove garlic, finely grated

Handful of lemon basil (roughly 10–15 leaves), slivered

Grated Parmigiano-Reggiano or local cheese with a hard and sharp profile, to garnish

From a bunch of beets, remove and discard all the stems. Keep the beet greens, discarding only the very heavy leaves and any that are unsightly. Set two beets aside and store the rest in a plastic bag in the refrigerator.

Boil the two beets until they can be easily pierced with a fork, approximately 40 to 45 minutes. Drain and let them cool, 20 minutes. Peel the beets and puree them in a high-powered food processor until smooth. To make the pasta dough, add 4 tablespoons (60 g) of the beet puree to the egg mixture in the Basic Pasta Dough recipe (page 16) and continue to follow the directions there for making, rolling out and cutting the dough for fettuccine.

Use the leftover beet puree as a garnish by adding a drizzle of cider vinegar (start with 1 teaspoon) and stir to combine. Taste and add more vinegar, if desired. Season with salt and pepper. Set aside for the flavors to combine.

Rinse the beet greens well. Drain and rinse once more. Spin or pat dry. Cut the greens into bite-sized pieces. Set aside.

Meanwhile, over low-medium heat, add the olive oil to a large 12-inch (30-cm) skillet. When the oil is hot and shimmery, add the red pepper flakes and toast for 1 minute. Reduce the heat to a simmer and add the beet greens and garlic. Toss the greens to coat them evenly. Cook until the greens are tender and wilted, 3 to 5 minutes, taking care to not burn the garlic. Turn off the heat. Set aside.

Bring a large pot of water to a boil. Generously salt the water and add the pasta. Fresh pasta cooks much faster than dry, usually in 1 to 2 minutes. Reserve ½ cup (120 ml) of the pasta water before draining. Drain well.

Add the pasta and ¼ cup (60 ml) of the reserved pasta water to the skillet with the beet greens and toss to coat. If necessary, add more pasta water and a drizzle of olive oil to loosen the pasta.

To serve, garnish with slivered lemon basil, a dollop of the beet puree, a generous drizzle of olive oil and freshly grated cheese.

Fresh Squid Ink Pasta with Clams, Garlic and Summer Tomatoes

Our summer days at the beach are long and lazy, and the seafood is always plentiful. In a culinary attempt to hold on to summer a little longer, I've elevated a typical seafood and pasta dish by adding squid ink to fresh pasta dough. The result is an inky black dough that adds a bit of drama and interest and a subtle flavor of the briny sea. I prefer the thicker cut of fettuccine for this dish; it holds well to the tomatoes and clams and its full body soaks up more of the robust broth. If you prefer a little less heat, simply reduce the amount of pepper flakes or omit altogether. Short on time? You can always substitute with dry squid ink pasta.

Serves 4–6

2 tsp (10 ml) squid ink (found in specialty markets or from a reputable online retailer)

Basic Pasta Dough (page 16)

¼ cup (60 ml) extra-virgin olive oil, plus more for serving

1 tsp Aleppo pepper (or substitute with ½ tsp red pepper flakes)

2 large cloves garlic, finely grated

½ cup (120 ml) Sauvignon Blanc

1 cup (250 g) crushed or pureed tomatoes (if using canned, San Marzano tomatoes are recommended)

⅓ cup (80 ml) chicken broth

Kosher salt and freshly ground pepper, to taste

15 fresh clams, scrubbed and cleaned

1 cup (150 g) peas, fresh or frozen

½ lb (225 g) cherry or grape tomatoes, halved or quartered if large

Fresh basil, to garnish

First prepare the fresh pasta by adding the squid ink to the egg mixture in the Basic Pasta Dough recipe (page 16), then proceed with the directions there for mixing, rolling out and cutting the dough into fettuccine or any long-shape pasta as desired.

When the dough is ready, bring a large pot of water to a boil.

In a large 12-inch (30-cm) skillet with deep sides over low–medium heat, warm the olive oil. When the oil is hot and shimmery, add the Aleppo pepper and let it sit until toasted, about 1 minute.

Add the garlic and stir until fragrant, 30 seconds. Remove the skillet from the heat to add the wine. Return to low–medium heat and simmer, 1 minute. Add the crushed tomatoes and broth. Season to taste with salt and pepper and stir to combine.

Raise the heat to medium, add the clams to the skillet and cover, cooking for 5 to 10 minutes, or until the clams have all opened. Add the peas and the tomato halves, gently stir to mix and cook to warm through, 1 to 2 minutes. Discard any clams that did not open. Turn off the heat and keep covered.

In the meantime, generously salt the boiling water and add the pasta, noting that fresh pasta cooks much faster than dry, usually within 1 to 2 minutes. Reserve ½ cup (120 ml) of the pasta water before draining. Drain well.

Add the pasta to the skillet, return to low heat and toss well to combine, about 1 minute. Add 2 tablespoons (30 ml) of the reserved pasta water, tossing again. If necessary, use more pasta water, a little at a time, to loosen the mixture. Garnish with fresh basil and a generous drizzle of olive oil and serve hot.

Cook's Notes: *The thickness of the pasta or substituting with dry pasta will affect how much broth is rendered in the pot at the end. If it is too brothy, simply serve in shallow bowls along with crusty bread to mop up all that wonderful liquid—it will appear intentional and no one will be the wiser!*

Fresh Fig and Goat Cheese Ravioli with Caramelized Figs

Figs fresh from the August harvest, caramelized with a dark balsamic butter sauce and strips of crispy prosciutto dress up homemade ravioli that has been stuffed with creamy goat cheese and a swirl of fig preserves. This is the perfect blend of sweet and savory. While time needs to be set aside to prepare homemade ravioli, nothing compares, and in my opinion, it is always worth the small effort. Homemade ravioli is so much lighter than frozen store-bought ravioli. Whenever pasta is prepared by your hands, something special happens—every fold, cut and crimp of dough becomes imprinted with your intentions and love for those you are serving.

Serves 4–6

10 oz (280 g) fresh herbed goat cheese, crumbled, room temperature

5 tbsp (100 g) fig jam or preserves

Basic Pasta Dough recipe (page 16)

5 thin slices Prosciutto di Parma

8 tbsp (115 g) butter

7–8 fresh Black Mission or Turkish figs, quartered through the stem

3 tbsp (45 ml) balsamic vinegar

1 tbsp (2 g) coarsely chopped fresh rosemary leaves

Freshly ground pepper, to taste

Kosher salt, to taste

You'll need a fluted ravioli cutter, a ravioli stamp (or a sharp knife), a pastry brush and a bowl of water.

Prepare the ravioli filling by gently mixing the goat cheese and fig preserves together, leaving streaks of both throughout. Set aside.

Follow the Basic Pasta Dough recipe (page 16), stopping when the dough has been rolled out to just thinner than 1⁄16 inch (1.6 mm)—any thinner and the dough will be compromised when stuffing. Dust two baking pans with flour and set aside.

Trim a long sheet of dough so that it has blunt edges and is approximately 5 inches (13 cm) wide and 15 inches (38 cm) long. Starting at approximately 1¼ inch (3 cm) from one end, place a tablespoon of the fig and goat cheese filling every 2½ inches (6 cm) down the center of the sheet of dough, stopping about halfway down the length of the dough. Lightly brush the water all around the edges of the dough and all around the filling. Brushing will help to seal the edges.

Fold the empty side of the dough over the filling, aligning the edges, and press down firmly around the filling and the edges to remove any air pockets and to create a firm seal.

Use the fluted side of a ravioli cutter, or a ravioli stamp, and trim the ravioli into even squares or circles, leaving approximately ¼ inch (6 mm) between the filling and the cut edge. Alternatively, use a sharp knife to cut the dough between the filling and press the edges firmly with the tines of a fork to seal. Repeat with the remaining sheets of dough. Transfer the stuffed ravioli to the dusted pans until ready.

Bring a large pot of water to a boil.

In the meantime, in a large 12-inch (30-cm) skillet over moderate heat, spread the prosciutto in a single layer, trying not to let the pieces touch, and cook until they begin to brown and shrivel, 3 to 5 minutes, careful not to burn, lowering the heat if necessary. Transfer the prosciutto to a paper towel-lined plate to absorb any excess oil and set aside.

In the same skillet over low-medium heat, carefully melt the butter. When the butter begins to foam, add the sliced figs, balsamic vinegar and the rosemary, and cook until the butter turns golden brown, the figs have begun to caramelize and the vinegar reduces and thickens, about 3 minutes. Season lightly with freshly ground pepper. Turn off the heat.

Meanwhile, generously salt the boiling water and add the ravioli. Fresh ravioli is done when they float to the top and will cook more quickly than frozen, so keep a watchful eye. Reserve ¼ cup (60 ml) of the pasta water before draining. Drain well.

Add the ravioli to the skillet with the figs. Add the reserved pasta water and turn the heat to low-medium, gently folding and tossing until the liquid emulsifies, 1 to 2 minutes.

To serve, divide into individual dishes. Top with broken pieces of prosciutto as well as a spoonful of any remaining balsamic-butter drizzled on top.

*See photo on page 140.

Cook's Notes: *Do not overcook the butter and balsamic mixture or it will begin to separate. Note that any residual tang from the balsamic will be cut when added to the goat cheese ravioli.*

ACKNOWLEDGMENTS

A raised glass and a most heartfelt THANK YOU to the many people who helped me author this cookbook—it really took a village, and I truly could not have accomplished this without you.

An acknowledgement first, and always, goes to God. For this and my many blessings, for giving me the strength, ability and knowledge to undertake this whole process and to persevere. For always giving me beauty for ashes.

To everyone at Page Street Publishing, especially my editor, Rebecca, thank you for reaching out to me with this amazing opportunity and for helping to shape this book. Your words are always so kind and thoughtful, and you are stellar at what you do. I value your input and suggestions wholeheartedly.

To Donaldson Farms, my "backyard farm," I am so grateful to your farmers and staff, and for your beautiful harvests. If I can't grow it, it will almost always come straight from your breathtaking fields. Thank you for your continued support of the blog and this cookbook. We are so fortunate to have you in our community.

Oliver and the staff at Harvest Drop, I thank you immensely for connecting me with the most beautiful ramps and zucchini blossoms, and for making sure I didn't miss the fleeting window of time for these wonderful ingredients. Oliver, you are an absolute pleasure to work with and a most generous soul—thank you so much for your help.

Arctic Foods and Amanda, I can't even begin to tell you how grateful I am to be able to avoid supermarket meats because of you. Thank you for providing us with superior, top-quality, locally raised meats. I'd be a vegetarian without you.

Valley Shepherd Creamery, thank you for your love of artisan cheese making and for sharing it with the rest of us. Thank you for gracing our corner of the world and for helping me to enhance these recipes with your incomparable products.

Mark Drabich and everyone at Metropolitan Seafood and Gourmet, thank you for setting out to New York City's Fulton Fish Market in the wee hours in the morning just to bring us fresh seafood every day. Quality matters, and I am grateful to you for helping to make some of these recipes possible.

At Orchard View Lavender Farm, thank you to Monica and Jim for your wonderful culinary lavender and for bringing the beauty of Provence to this part of New Jersey.

(continued)

To Well-Sweep Herb Farm, thank you for providing me with the most beautiful herbs. My garden and these recipes are better because of you.

To the recipe testers who went to work in their kitchens, all over the world, to make certain these recipes were dependable, I truly could not have done this without you and your valuable feedback. Thank you sincerely Katie Brewster, Skye Carlsen, Antonia Cattaneo, Colleen Chodkiewicz, Bobby DeKleine, Veronica Dimitriadis, Diana Gray, Sarah Groszewski, Shannon Gunther, Maxie James, Val Jorgensen, Kathleen McBreen, Lisa Quinn O'Flaherty and budding foodie Sam Quinn O'Flaherty.

To Mom, for always being the first one to taste-test a recipe, for your honest feedback, for reminiscing with me and for being the shoulder I lean on quite often. I love you.

To Tom, for being my husband and for never complaining when I send you out for last-minute ingredients, sometimes (often) several times in a day—thank you and sorry! For your honest feedback and for always taking the initiative to clean up the mess I make in the kitchen so that I can tend to the kids, take my photos or just relax—I appreciate all you do for us. I love you.

Giada and Anthony, you are the greatest loves of my life. Giada, you carry so many of your great-grandmother's traits; she would have enjoyed your personality immensely. Thank you for your willingness to try almost everything I make. Your help in proofreading the recipes was spot-on too, what an eye for detail! Anthony, my reluctant taste-tester, thank you for being my assistant photographer and for giving me encouragement and sweet notes tucked into my work binders and around the house—you're such a thoughtful little soul. I love you both with all my heart.

ABOUT THE AUTHOR

Nikki Marie is the creator of Chasing the Seasons, a food blog she authors about seasonal living and home cooking in rural New Jersey. Her recipes and food photography have been featured in many online publications, were nominated for the 2017 Saveur Blog Award (Best New Voice category) and have been recognized by the New Jersey State Department of Agriculture's Jersey Fresh Love campaign. Her appreciation and love of food, especially Italian food, was inspired early on by her grandmother and later through her travels to Tuscany. Nikki resides in northwest New Jersey with her husband and two children.

Find her at:
www.chasingtheseasons.com

Instagram: chasingtheseasons

INDEX